Guide to Basic News Writing

Melvin Mencher
Columbia University

wcb

WM. C. BROWN COMPANY PUBLISHERS
Dubuque, Iowa

CONTENTS

PREFACE

Guide to Basic News Writing is designed to help you
use Basic News Writing and the accompanying workbook.
Guide summarizes the major points in each chapter in
the textbook and includes sample stories for the
exercises.

Workbook: Basic News Writing plunges students into the realities of journalism at once. Stories are
identified by slug. Documents from various sources
are used. Most of the exercises are based on actual
events, and the stories that reporters wrote are included in Guide. Students want to see how the pro-
fessionals do it, and you can give them the opportunity to compare their work with that of the men and
women in the field.

Although the workbook was structured to follow
the textbook chapter by chapter, you may want to
select exercises and other work from various sections
of Workbook. Please browse through it and choose
the material that seems best suited to your course.
There are plenty of exercises, enough for several
writing assignments a week. You may want to assign
some writing to be done at home as well. For home
assignments, students can be asked to consult reference materials.

Each chapter in the textbook has two purposes:
To review important points that have been made and
to introduce new ideas. These ideas and concepts
are introduced in a realistic setting. That is, reporters are shown applying them to actual situations.
This approach can be seen in the first chapter where
several young journalists are shown handling news
stories. Although there is no apparent instruction
in news writing, a number of principles are introduced, and these are later discussed in detail.

The examples, anecdotes and illustrations have been selected to give the textbook the human interest that is characteristic of good journalism.

By staying with some of the reporters introduced in early chapters, I hope to give the student a feeling of intimacy with the journalists he or she is reading about. In the first chapter, we see Lindy Washburn covering a fire for AP. In subsequent chapters, the questions that Washburn asked her sources are discussed to show the student something about news values.

In the second chapter, several grim photographs are used to illustrate the fact that journalists must be prepared to handle unpleasant events. In the chapter on taste, the student is asked to examine these pictures again. The pictures may have won a Pulitzer Prize for photography, but they are obviously offensive. What principles can be derived from their use to guide us in matters of taste?

Learning to write is not easy. An editor of Fortune magazine said that anyone who brags that writing is easy is either a bad liar or an unregenerate liar. But learning to write does not have to be as difficult as it is said to be. I have tried to reduce the mysteries of journalistic writing to a few concepts. Once mastered, these will give the student confidence at the typewriter.

Poor spelling and grotesque grammar get in the way of journalism instruction. If you find that you prefer to begin your journalism instruction with drills in language, use the skill drills in chapter 10. Some instructors prefer students to relax at the beginning of the course, and they set their students to writing without too much instruction in these subjects.

But no instructor should tolerate sloppy writing. Years ago, a journalism instructor passed on to me this iron-clad rule for copy:

You are permitted two errors in spelling, two in punctuation and two in grammar. On the third error for any of these, I stop reading, mark the paper a failure and return it. The failing grade will be removed on submission of a rewritten paper, handed in within a week, with no errors in any category. A misspelled name is an automatic failure.

You may want to give your students more or less leeway. With this rule in force, students soon learn to consult a dictionary and a book on grammar. You may want to add stylebook errors to the list.

Instructors have suggested that these basic standards be set for stories:

1. ACCURACY. The writing should conform to the facts of the exercise or event.
2. TRUTHFUL EXPRESSION. The language should be faithful to the facts, neither exaggerated nor distorted. Cliches, inappropriate colloquialisms and trite expressions do not belong in the news story.

In the early weeks, you might try talking stories through with students. That is, before the students are to write, you might have them think aloud how they will approach the facts given in the exercises. You should ask what the most important or unusual aspect of the material is, the next in importance, and so on. This will give the student a sense of story structure.

The idea is to have the student learn to think as a journalist. In these days when linear thinking is supposed to be a relic of the past, the student may be surprised to learn that most news stories are linear, that they march in a straight line from beginning (most significant or unusual element) to the end (least important, summary or surprise ending).

There is, of course, no single way to write any news story. But there are many wrong ways. Students need to be shown that most badly written stories are the result of imprecise thinking.

The workbook that accompanies <u>Basic News Writing</u> is based on <u>Workbook: News Reporting and Writing</u>, which is also published by Wm. C. Brown Company Publishers. Instructors who want additional exercises for their students might want to consult this workbook.

I welcome your suggestions and comments. Journalism is a group enterprise. Pulling together, staffers put out newspapers and news broadcasts with amazing speed, accuracy and effectiveness. I think we can do the same for journalism instruction. Many of the ideas in the text and the workbook have been suggested by colleagues. I would be delighted to have yours for future editions.

PART 1   JOURNALISTS IN ACTION

1   IN THE NEWSROOM AND ON THE BEAT

The newsroom and beat scenes in this chapter are designed to put students into the working world of the
journalist. You might want to discuss with your students any questions about reporting and writing that
they have. I hope that you will emphasize the truism
about journalism--journalists write reporting.

One of the pitfalls into which beginning students fall--and some news writing texts--is that they
presume the purpose of news writing is the perfectly
written story. That's a half-truth. The purpose is
to produce a story that matches the event being described. Writing is too often seen by youngsters as
an end in itself.

To summarize the points of chapter 1, they are:

1. Journalists write reporting.
2. News is gathered in several ways: from on-the-
    spot observation, by telephone, from documents
    and records, from the wire services.
3. The basic news values are importance, the unusual
    or exceptional, prominence.

WORKBOOK

For the students' first writing assignment, try some
of the exercises beginning on page EXERCISES I: DE-
VELOPING THE STORY IDEA. I suggest that you talk
through a few of the exercises before the students
start to write. You might put their suggestions for
the important ideas on the blackboard. Then you can
circle the one the class agrees is the best theme for
the lead, numbering all ideas in order of importance.

1

EXERCISES I: DEVELOPING THE STORY IDEA

Numbers in parentheses indicate the order of the
ideas as they should be used in the story. Here are
the ideas to look for:

A. MEMORIAL: Softball game to be played Sunday for
    memorial fund.
B. ZOO: (1) Birth control being considered for
    tigers at the zoo. (2) An elephant and a burro
    have been purchased. (3) Name-the-burro con-
    test announced.
C. LAUNDROMAT: Naked man arrested in laundromat.
    (Humorous leads encouraged.)
D. WEATHER: (1) Temperature reached a 15-year low
    of 25 this morning. (2) Three-day cold snap
    expected to end today. (The order could be re-
    versed at the instructor's discretion, or (1)
    and (2) put in a single-sentence lead.)
E. FIRE: (1) Wife rescued man who fell asleep in
    car listening to baseball game. (2) A&P blaze.
F. OMBUDSMAN:

        Bruce Stroh, a former local high school
    basketball player who served five years in the
    state penitentiary for armed robbery, today
    was appointed state ombudsman for the state's
    penal institutions.

    If the students have trouble grasping the tech-
nique of reducing events to an essential idea or major theme, then try EXERCISES II: FINDING THE THEME.

EXERCISES II: FINDING THE THEME

A. Dispute

As given, the facts resemble the chronological approach that beginning journalism students use in writing their stories. The last sentence, the chief's
resignation, should be underlined or circled. The
lead might be:

> Police Chief Lloyd Earl resigned last
> night in the midst of a controversy between
> him and the Queens Mountain Rescue Squad.

B. Taxes

Again, the key is in the last sentence. Although the
proposed budget, which is revealed for the first time,
is important, readers and listeners will want to know
how it will affect them. (This approach - the effect
of events on individuals - underlies much of the copy
in the manual.) Some possible beginnings:

> County Manager David Hunscher told the
> county Board of Commissioners last night that
> taxes probably will have to be raised next
> year to meet expenditures in the new budget.
> The budget, which Hunscher submitted to
> the commissioners last night, totals $54.8
> million. This is $2.1 million higher than
> the current budget.

Or:

> Gaston County is in a financial pinch,
> and taxes will probably have to be raised to
> keep the county in a sound financial position.
> In so many words, this is what County
> Manager David Hunscher told the Gaston County
> Board of Commissioners last night when he

3

presented his proposed $54.8 million budget for 1976-77.

C. Mail

The possible change in the mail delivery schedule is the obvious lead. In this story, the assistant post-master general obviously speaks for the service, and his name need not be placed in the lead, unless you prefer to emphasize extreme caution in attribution at this stage. A possible lead:

> The postal service is considering cutting home mail delivery back to two days a week and business mail delivery to three times a week.
> T.J. Ellingson, an assistant U.S. post-master general, said today that the cutback in deliveries is one of several plans to save costs....

Or:

> An assistant U.S. postmaster general said today that the postal service is considering cutting....

D. Shooting

> Bernice Joyce, 32, of 101 Rebecca Drive, was charged with attempted homicide this morn-ing following a domestic quarrel in which her husband was shot and critically wounded.

EXERCISES III: GUIDELINES FOR EDITING COPY

Three exercises in copy editing for marking copy are included in chapter 1 of the workbook.

Chapter 10 of the textbook contains the copy editing symbols and has examples of how they are used. Sally Grimes, who teaches copy editing at the University of Massachusetts, has designed an exercise you might want to try with your students before they do the workbook exercises.

You can distribute version 1, and after the students have worked on it, distribute version 2. You can make the learning easier by retaining the number guides when you hand out the first version.

Version 1

1
MIAMI, Dec.10 - "Why does God hate me?" Alan McDonald
                            2
asked from his hospital bed
                            3
    "When the gun powder went off, I couldn't believe
                                                    4
it. I said, No, God couldn't do this to me again."
    5   6
    Mr. McDonald, 23 years old, lay in serious con-
                                7
dition in the burn ward of Miami's Jakson Memorial

Hospital for the second time in his life severely
        8
burned.
                            9
    In February 1966, Mr.MacDonald was doused with

flaming gasoline by a playmate. He was massively

burned and disfigured. It took skin grafts from an

older brother and years of plastic surgery to restore
                    10
his horribly charred body.

Last week, on an Everglades hunting trip with friends Mr. McDonald was squatting over a bowl of gun-

11

powder near a smoldering campfire, making 6 bullets to save money.

12

The fire sudenly popped. A spark ignited the gunpowder.

13

"I didn't realize what happened at first", he

14

recounted.

15

"And then I heard the sound from thirteen years

16

ago. I was burning. I ruled to put out the fire and

17   18

I thought, 'Oh, God not again'."

19

His compansionshelped quench the fire and strug-

gled with him to the nearest road, where a passing

20   21   22

florida Trooper called an ambulance. "If my friend

23

hadn't been there, I would have hjumped into a canal

24

with a rock around my neck," McDonald despaired.

Version 2

1

MIAMI, Dec.10 - "Why does God Hate me?" Alan McDonald

2

asked from his hospital bed

"When the gun powder went off, I couldn't believe
it. I said, No, God couldn't do this to me again."

Mr. McDonald, 23 years old, lay in serious condition in the burn ward of Miami's Jakson Memorial
Hospital for the second time in his life severely
burned.

In February 1966, Mr. MacDonald was doused with
flaming gasoline by a playmate. He was massively
burned and disfigured. It took skin grafts from an
older brother and years of plastic surgery to restore
his horribly charred body.

Last week, on an Everglades hunting trip with
friends, Mr. McDonald was squatting over a bowl of
gunpowder near a smoldering campfire, making 6 bullets
to save money.

The fire suddenly popped. A spark ignited the
gunpowder.

"I didn't realize what happened at first," he
recounted.

7

"And then I heard the sound from (thirteen) years

ago. I was burning. I rolled to put out the fire and

I thought, 'Oh, God not again.'"

His companions helped quench the fire and strug-

gled with him to the nearest road, where a passing

florida trooper called an ambulance. "If my friend

hadn't been there, I would have jumped into a canal

with a rock around my neck," McDonald despaired.

---

1. Paragraph mark, also c/lc. ∟

2. Period. ⊗

3. Bring together. ⌣

4. This is correct punctuation for a quote within
   a quote.

5. Style. Some papers such as The New York Times
   do use honorifics. Most do not except in obit-
   uaries. Delete.

6. Style. Again, either is possible. Be sure to
   make copy conform to individual paper's style.
   Delete, close up.

7. Insert letter. ∧

8. Transpose. ⌐∟

9. Name misspelled: reread names with special
   attention. Delete letter, close up. ⌒

10. Delete judgmental adverbs and adjectives. Close
    up.

11. Spell out. ○

8

12. Spelling. When in doubt, use the dictionary. Substitute word. ⌣⤳

13. Commas and periods go inside quotes. Transpose. ⧖

14. Stick to "said" in attributing quotes. Substitute word.

15. Contract to figure. ⬭

16. Watch for typographical errors.

17. Insert comma. ⋏

18. Transpose. ⧖

19. Separate. |

20. Uppercase. ≡

21. Lowercase. ╱

22. Paragraph mark. ∟

23. Delete letter. ℓ

24. Stick to "said."

Should you want to start the students on grammar, punctuation and spelling early, chapter 10 in the Guide has the suggested answers to the workbook exercises.

This chapter digs more deeply into the character and
personality of the journalist than did chapter 1,
which showed journalists at work. I have selected a
wide range of journalists - men and women, beginners
and veteran reporters, those who respond to the excitement of journalism, and those who are in the field
because they want to help others through journalism.

For students thinking of journalism as a major
and possibly as a career, this chapter should show
students what will be asked of them. You might stress
the fact that working journalists work. I don't think
there is much sense in misleading students about the
demands journalism places on its people.

Students should discover that for most journalists
the desire to work and to excel comes from within, that
the journalist needs no one standing over his or her
shoulder with a whip, a snarl or a threat.

Journalists enjoy their work, and I hope you can
convey that sense of excitement and pleasure. You
might select stories in local newspapers for discussion and invite the reporters who have written them
to speak to your class. The students will find the
reporters' enthusiasm contagious.

WORKBOOK

When I was field testing Basic News Writing at Humboldt State University in California, I found that
many beginners had trouble finding the lead. They
struggled in the early weeks and often wrote general
rather than specific leads. The two exercises I discovered to be most useful in illustrating how leads
are written are A. GOLFERS and B. CHANGES in EXER-
CISES I.

EXERCISES I

A. Golfers

Students can easily understand that Sally's hole in
one shot is the most important event of the day when
you point out that it is the first such shot in five
years and that the last was by a professional golfer.
They should also be told that they must include in
the lead some identifying label that tells the reader
Sally is a local girl.
    The lead is the local golfer's hole-in-one,
followed by the fact that she is in a tie for second
place in the opening round. Play up the quotes. Remind students that good quotes make good stories.
    Here is how Sam Archibald, of the University of
Colorado, handles this story as a teaching device:

       WHO: Eisenhower High School senior Sally
    Grubbs sank a hole-in-one at the State Women's
    Golf Tournament today.
       WHAT: The first hole-in-one by a woman on
    the Freeport Golf Course in five years was
    shot today by Sally Grubbs, an Eisenhower ....
       WHEN: Just before dusk last night, Sally
    Grubbs sank a hole-in-one and took second
    place....
       WHERE: The seventh hole at Freeport Golf
    Course was the scene of what is the first hole-
    in-one by a woman on the course in five years.
       WHY: Because her seven-year-old sister
    gave her good luck, Eisenhower High School stu-
    dent Sally Grubbs says she was able to sink a
    hole-in-one in the ....
       HOW: Hitting the ball right on the line
    and having her kid sister stand by for luck
    gave Sally Grubbs a hole-in-one at ....

B. Changes

When <u>Workbook</u> was written, the lead clearly was that a local teacher is quitting to drive a bus because he says his salary is too low. But when it was tested, Poland had been in the news. The Communist government had instituted martial law. Clearly, the teacher who joined the school faculty from Warsaw was the lead, and some students saw this. You might tell the students this incident to demonstrate how news values shift with events.

Most of the students, however, had neither the bus driver nor the teacher from Poland in their leads. The typical lead read this way:

> School Superintendent Herbert Gilkeyson has announced personnel changes for next year in the school system.

You might want to show them why this kind of lead is not considered sound by journalists. Obviously, you do not want to rush them on the subject since lead writing is discussed in detail in chapter 8. But they should have some idea now of what a lead is. The examples in chapter 1 of reporters at work should have helped give the students a general idea that the lead contains the most important or significant aspect of the event.

I also found that students have a tendency to swallow press releases and publicity handouts. You might try C. BELMONT in an early session to show students the dangers of stenographic journalism. At Humboldt, many students accepted all the superlatives of the releases. Here is a typical lead:

> Television star Buster C. Rabbe and the vivacious Hollywood beauty, starlet Holly (Kitten) Grove, will be among the many stars and prominent athletes to appear next month at the underwater film extravaganza at the Belmont Hotel.

Grove is given considerable attention. Her various beauty awards are detailed. I should say that no one used her measurements, a sign of progress. But the adjectives and the naivete abounded.

EXERCISES II: FINDING THE THEME

EXERCISES II includes additional work in finding the theme. Again, you might have the students first select the theme. Then they should be asked to put the other facts in order, from most to least important. Then they can write.

A. Drive

The local chapter of the American Civil Liberties Union today began a membership drive it hopes will save the chapter from collapse.

B. Gas

The Wisconsin Gas Co. today halted all further gas and industrial hookups in central and eastern Wisconsin.
In addition, the utility proposed to the state Public Service Commission a plan to reduce natural gas deliveries to some present customers during temporary shortages.
The utility acted after the state Public Service Commission warned....

C. Tennis

Here, one of the guidelines to news--prominence--applies:

Billie Jean King will take part in the 12th annual Freeport Tennis Clinic Aug. 21-24.
The internationally known tennis star will play two matches before local audiences Aug. 23. She will....

D. Bicycle Trip

A University of Rochester medical student will ride his bicycle across the United States for science this summer.

Edward A. Nelson, of Kent, Conn., is undertaking the project to measure the body's ability to adapt to intensive training....

E. Guns

A national organization that seeks to ban handguns intends to try to unseat Rep. William Trenzier because of his opposition to federal handgun legislation.

The threat was made last night by Albert Waring, an official in Washington, D.C., of the National Coalition to Ban Handguns. He spoke to some 150 persons at a meeting....

NOTE: There is enough information for an entire story here, if you want to assign one.

F. Brush-Off

Baseball is getting too sedate for Sparky Anders.

Asked what he thought of the warning to managers to cool off players who lately have been fighting, Anders says baseball can be "too safe."

"I think you have to...."

This chapter gets down to the business of news writing. As an introduction to news values, you might have your students clip five or ten stories from the local newspaper and make the following analysis:
Classify the story according to the probable reason it was used:

A. Importance or significance
B. Unusual or exceptional
C. Prominence of person involved

This should give the student a good start toward developing a news sense.
To make instruction complete, I suggest a second analysis with the same clippings. See how many of these news story leads:

A. Center on a person
B. Center on an event

The reason I suggest this second analysis is that it will help the student to write a lead. The first analysis tells the student why the event is worth covering and how much he or she should write. The second analysis starts the student writing.
These analyses are important in another way. They should demonstrate to the student that thinking precedes writing, that the news writer must plan. It may not be a bad idea for you to allow students to make brief outlines of the news stories you assign them to write--if they can be helped by such a procedure.
I've found that students rely on their outline making for a while and then find it unnecessary as their skill increases. I know that some instructors do not like to allow their students to outline a

15

piece. But I can't condemn what I do myself. In writing long pieces, I find an outline helpful to keep me on track. So do a lot of professional writers I know.

The opening incident of the chapter, the suit against Santa Claus, did indeed happen. It was related to me by a courthouse reporter. I use this illustration to open the chapter because students must learn quickly the two sides to journalism--its somber face when it is concerned with stories of importance, and its light-hearted visage when it handles unusual events.

WORKBOOK

If you want additional work in identifying news values why not begin with the exercises that were not used in chapter 2, and then try the exercises in this chapter. Have students list for each exercise the news values involved:

Importance

Unusual or exceptional

Prominence

Proximity

Timeliness

Conflict

Currency

For the stories you want them to write as their laboratory exercise work in this chapter, first have them decide whether the story will focus on an individual or an event. This second analysis results in:

A. Craftsman - A person.
B. Poet - An event.
C. Answer - A person (commenting on an event).

D. Violence - An event.
E. Center - An event.
F. Psychiatrist - A person (saying something about a situation).

The next step is the story. A, B, C and E are easier to handle than the others. Use your judgment.

EXERCISES

A. Craftsman

John D'Mura, 13, of Flagstaff, has won second place in the junior division of the Fisher Craftsman's Guild Scholarship contest.
He received a $4,000 college scholarship for his model car design....

This is an example of localizing a story. The piece can be written in three paragraphs. You might discuss with the class whether it is necessary to list any other names. Of what interest are teenagers from Medford and Arlington to your readers?

B. Poet

Bergen County Court Judge Harvey Smith combined poetry with the law yesterday and overturned a state statute which makes it illegal to utter obscenities on the telephone.

His decision, written entirely in rhyme, reverses a lower court conviction of a 28-year-old man who used a common four-letter expletive when he told the Ridgefield Park court clerk to perform a sexual act on herself. Smith's decision affects the illegality of obscene phone calls.

In his verse decision, Judge Smith twice used an abbreviated form of expletive.

The five-page opinion concludes:

Statutory attempts
to regulate
pure bluster....
                    -The Record,
Bergen County, N.J.

Another beginning:

A Bergen County Court Judge turned to verse in an opinion handed down yesterday in which he held obscenities are protected by the first amendment.

In 15 stanzas of rhymed couplets, Judge Harvey Smith ruled....

This story brings out the poet in some students. Fred S. Kempe wrote this lead:

A man swore at Geraldine over the phone,
And she thought things couldn't be worse.
Until the judge told her it wasn't a crime,
And he did it quite smartly in verse.

A more straightforward lead with a bit of clever phrasing was written by Rob Fleder:

County Court Judge Harvey Smith yesterday reversed the profanity conviction of a Ridgefield Park man in a poetic 15-stanza decision that said the lower court ruling had neither rhyme nor reason.

The use of obscenities in print is worth discussing. Here, the judge wrote F---, and the reporter was even more restrained ("a common four-letter expletive"). Why not use the judge's abbreviation?

C. Answer

The Record used all of this short poem, despite the
obviously tasteless dash. This story should be handled in a straightforward manner. It is dangerous
to try to be humorous on matters of taste. The
judge's opinion, on the other hand, seems to be no
more than a light-hearted handling of an interesting
legal issue.

D. Violence

Here is one way to handle this story:

> CHICAGO - A study conducted by a major
> advertising agency indicates that violent
> television programs are leading some viewers
> to boycott the sponsors' products.
> The study, conducted by the J. Walter
> Thompson Company, was revealed here today at
> the annual conference of the American Adver-
> tising Federation.
> John Donaldson, a vice-president of the
> agency, said a sample of adult viewers con-
> cluded that:
> Ten percent....
> Eight percent....
> The findings could cause advertisers to
> shift their programming, several of those at-
> tending the convention said. Frank Denton
> of....(Quote him).

E. Center

> Four local merchants who have stores on
> the site of the proposed Salvation Army Com-
> munity Center last night asked the Zoning
> and Planning Board to refuse approval of the
> center.

The army has asked for a go-ahead to build a $500,000 two-story building at 740 Elm St. The land was promised the army as part of a deal in which the present center would be torn down for the proposed mall. The swap is part of the city's downtown renewal project.

The merchants said they would lose their businesses if the board approved the construction.

"We cannot...." (Quote Berents and name the merchants. Quote Major Geddings.)

F. Psychiatrist

Dr. Raymond Hertell, chief of psychiatry at the local Whitney-Painter Clinic, says that the popularity of the Unifying Church among young people is no cause for alarm.

The church, which demands unswerving obedience, has successfully recruited among young men and women, many of whom have severed their ties to family and friends.

"Really, this is nothing new," said Dr. Hertell, a nationally known psychiatrist. "The church fosters a repudiation of...."

Dr. Hertell's comments were made in a letter to the editor of this newspaper and in an interview.

PART 2   REPORTING

4 FINDING INFORMATION AND GATHERING FACTS

This chapter gives the student a closer look at the
reporting process. I stress the need for students to
observe events directly, whenever possible. There is
too much telephone reporting these days. The essential point for news writing is that the directly observed event leads to a livelier, more accurate and
more interesting story.

In addition to direct observation, the chapter
stresses the reporter's need to know a great deal, how
things work and the role reference books and background material play in good news writing. It might
not be a bad idea to talk about how a few governmental
processes work--your city government, the administration of the college or university, the court system
in town and so on.

(Incidentally, I was the reporter who did not
know what a barrow is. I had that harrowing experience covering the State Fair in Albuquerque, N.M.,
as a young reporter.)

To force their students to keep up with events
by reading newspapers and listening to the news on
television and radio, some instructors regularly give
current events quizzes.

A good idea for helping students feel at home in
the library is to have the reference librarian give
them a tour, pointing out where the essential references are kept and how to use them.

WORKBOOK

For exercises using reference works, try SKILL DRILLS
I and II.

SKILL DRILL I: QUALITY

This is a good library exercise to use to introduce
students to references works. They need only consult
the latest volume of the Statistical Abstract of the
United States. You can make the exercise a little
more challenging by asking them to look back five
and/or 10 years for progress or decline in these categories for your state. Since the listings are usually numbered, it would be easy for the student to see
relative standings for the most recent year, five
years ago and 10 years ago. Most of the figures in
the workbook are for 1980.

SKILL DRILL II: REFERENCES is probably easier
to handle as all of these reference books are usually
kept in libraries or are readily available. Certainly, all students should be acquainted with The World
Almanac, Reader's Guide, and Who's Who in America.
And they should be taught how to use The New York
Times Index or Facts on File.

SKILL DRILL II: REFERENCES

A. The World Almanac.
B. Who's Who in America.
C. Books in Print.
D. The New York Times Index; FBI Uniform Crime
    Reports.
E. The New York Times Index; Reader's Guide to
    Periodical Literature.
F. Bartlett's Familiar Quotations; the play itself.
G. An encyclopedia.
H. A world atlas.
I. The World Almanac.
J. The World Almanac.
K. The city directory.
L. The National Zip Code & Post Office Directory.

M. The New York Times Index; the morgue of the
   local newspaper; Reader's Guide.
N. The state legislative reference service or a
   similar agency in the state capital.
O. A road atlas.

SKILL DRILL III: ARITHMETIC

Some instructors insist that their students learn
basic arithmetic, if they do not already know how to
handle percentages, fractions and other simple tasks.
SKILL DRILL III: ARITHMETIC is a good diagnostic
tool. It will tell your students how well they can
handle basic arithmetic.

Percentages

A. The increase is 300. Placing the increase over
   the original figure of 1,300 gives 300/1,300,
   which equals 23%.
B. The increase is 3,700, which is divided by the
   preceding year's total of 15,025 to give the
   rounded-off figure of 25%.
C. 83%.
D. 38%.
E. Today's texts are 200 pages; a decade ago they
   were 350 pages. 200/350 equals 57%.

Fractions

A. 4/15 equals about one-fourth.
B. 265/850 equals one-third; 165/850 equals one-
   fifth.
C. Three times as many....
D. Three-fourths.
E. One-tenth (rounded off).

Rates

A. 8% X $1,000,000 or .08 X $1,000,000, equals $80,000.
B. $500,000/$5,500,000 equals 1/11 or 9%.
C. $3,900.
D. 7% of $2,000,000 is $140,000; 7.5% of $2,000,000
   is $150,000, which would mean $10,000 a year more
   ...or $200,000 over the life....
D. Rate X time equals distance........... R X t = D
   Rate X ½ hour equals 47 miles......... R X ½ = 47
   Rate/2 equals 47 miles, or .... $\frac{R}{2}$ = 47
   Rate equals 47 X 2.................... R = 47 X 2
   Rate equals 94 miles per hour .... R = 94

My students have found that the most difficult
questions to be: Percentages, D and E; Fractions, E;
Rates, D. When the skill drill was used by Professor
Arthur M. Sanderson, of the University of South Florida at Tampa, the students averaged four to five errors.
Those questions giving the students the most diffi-
culty were: Percentages, B and E; Fractions, E; Rates,
all but C.

Professor Sanderson suggests that you may wish to
discuss the use of the hand calculator. I would recommend its use for reporters who are unable to do
basic computations. The only calculator a student
will need for reporting is one with four functions -
addition, subtraction, multiplication and division.
A basic knowledge of arithmetic is necessary, however,
to work the calculator. As Professor Sanderson puts
it, "You have to know the gazinta," or what goes into
what.

If your students do not fare too well, take
heart. Here are a couple of mathematical gems from
The New York Times published during the summer of
1976:

White Plains, for example, had no homicides last year, but has had one so far in 1976. That is an increase of 100 percent.

Mount Lebanon...did not have a single robbery in 1974, but there were three last year, producing an increase of 300 percent.

As you know, 100 percent of zero is zero, and 300 percent of zero is still zero.

For a challenging assignment in building background, try SKILL DRILL IV: FAMOUS WORKS. Some instructors take 10 or 15 of these works and assign students the task of looking them up in reference works. This usually does the job of familiarizing them with a variety of references.

SKILL DRILL IV: FAMOUS WORKS

1. Plato
2. Homer
3. Shakespeare
4. Tolstoy
5. James Joyce
6. Dylan Thomas
7. T. S. Eliot
8. The Beatles
9. Henrik Ibsen
10. Samuel Taylor Coleridge
11. Nathanael West
12. Virgil
13. J. D. Salinger
14. J. R. R. Tolkien
15. Orson Welles
16. Dostoevski
17. Beethoven
18. Mozart
19. Verdi
20. Fedirico Fellini
21. Tennessee Williams
22. Thomas Hardy
23. Oswald Spengler
24. F. Scott Fitzgerald
25. Thomas Mann
26. Jane Austen
27. Claude Debussy
28. William Faulkner
29. Ernest Hemingway
30. Theodore Dreiser
31. Anton Chekhov
32. Voltaire
33. Nathaniel Hawthorne
34. Emily Brontë
35. Gilbert and Sullivan
36. Herman Melville
37. Sherwood Anderson
38. Walt Whitman
39. Charles Darwin
40. Charles Dickens
41. W. Somerset Maugham
42. Henry James
43. Albert Camus
44. Andrew Marvell
45. Lewis Carroll
46. Cervantes

47. Gustave Flaubert	73. St. Paul
48. Leonardo Da Vinci	74. Hector Berlioz
49. Pablo Picasso	75. Marcel Proust
50. D. W. Griffith	76. Lincoln Steffens
51. Adolph Hitler	77. John Locke
52. John Dos Passos	78. Emile Zola
53. Agatha Christie	79. Martin Luther
54. John Keats	80. Richard Wright
55. Joseph Heller	81. Franz Schubert
56. Henry Fielding	82. Aristotle
57. Shakespeare	83. St. Augustine
58. Aristophanes	84. Igor Stravinsky
59. Eugene O'Neill	85. René Descartes
60. Henry David Thoreau	86. Ernest Hemingway
61. Henry Ford	87. Henry Luce
62. Sigmund Freud	88. Eli Whitney
63. Henry Adams	89. George Bernard Shaw
64. Richard Wagner	90. D. H. Lawrence
65. Elizabeth Barrett Browning	91. Aldous Huxley
	92. Margaret Mead
66. Goethe (Or Gounod, the composer of the opera "Faust.")	93. James T. Farrell
	94. John Steinbeck
	95. Jesus
67. Abraham Lincoln	96. Walter Scott
68. Edmund Spenser	97. Upton Sinclair
69. Karl Marx	98. Charlotte Brontë
70. James Watt	99. Adam Smith
71. Tschaikowsky	100. Beethoven
72. Franz Kafka	

EXERCISE

For writing work, try A. GROWTH. This is the kind of story college newspapers often run. It should demonstrate the usefulness of mathematical proficiency.

A. Growth

A couple of the relevant figures the student should derive on his or her own are the student-faculty ratio and the average amount of aid per student. In the former case, the ratio seems to have held at 13.6-to-1. Aid per student has increased from $1,868 to $2,563, an increase of 37 percent, whereas tuition has increased 100 percent. The growth in assets should be calculated also.

The student probably should lead with the idea of a decade of progress but the necessity to initiate a fund drive for the library addition.

The president's statement about the need for more money for student assistance should be high up, and that section should include the figures on student assistance per capita today and 10 years ago.

Robert L. Walker, the president of Mallory College, today reported the college has increased its net assets by 86 percent over the past 10 years to $47,882,299.

He called the period a decade of progress. But he said much remains to be done.

"We are faced with ever-increasing demands on our plant," he said in a statement accompanying the release of comparative figures for the 10-year period.

He said the college's "first priority...."

ASSIGNMENT

To excite your students about research, try this "Where are they now?" assignment.

Have the students examine the yearbook and news stories of the graduating class of five, 10, or 15 years ago. Find the students considered the brightest, the most likely to succeed, the leading athletes. What has happened to them?

The first part of the assignment is not too difficult, but finding out where they are and what they are doing now may take some digging. Students will have to check the alumni office, department heads, coaches and, if possible, the clipping file of the local newspaper. Some, of course, may be in one of the volumes of Who's Who. Others may have sunk out of sight, and that, too, is interesting.

The concept introduced in this chapter for developing
ideas for the news story before and during the reporting may be difficult at first. But I think the examples I give should make it understandable and acceptable.
       Most people, including journalism students,
believe that journalists get the lead or main idea
for their stories only after digging out the facts,
making observations, reading documents. This is true
to a point. The whole truth is that there is not
enough time to dig out all the facts, to make every
relevant observation and to read all the documents.
Journalists cannot function unless they have a few
ideas that will guide them on the story.
       The reporter who does not take to the event some
ideas before reporting is as lost as the news writer
who begins his or her piece without any idea of the
lead - and this is just the parallel I hope you will
draw for your students. We cannot operate in journalism without planning and thinking before reporting
and writing.
       The concept presented in this chapter is the re-
sult of interviews and observations I made several
years ago for another textbook. I have written arti-
cles about this reporting process and it is accepted
as the basic description of this process.

       A good way to demonstrate the reporting process
is to ask the students what comes to mind if they are
told to cover:

1. A fire in a student dormitory.
2. A fire in a college gymnasium at 3 a.m.
3. A fire in a grain elevator.
4. A fire in a factory using a toxic substance.

Ask them to list their first thoughts. Generally, students will think as follows:

1. Was anyone hurt or killed?
2. What caused a fire to start at that hour?
3. How did it start; how much damage was done?
4. Has the substance spread; will it endanger the community?

These are the first questions a reporter asks. They are his or her ideas, generated before leaving the newsroom. They are the basis of the reporting. The answers to these questions often become the lead to the story.

1. A fire in a student dormitory on the Wheeling College Campus last night took the lives of three students and injured 18 other students.
2. A fire of unknown origin damaged some 250 seats in the Wheeling College gymnasium early this morning.
3. The Albert Bros. grain elevator 12 miles west of the city burst into flames at 11 a.m. today and preliminary estimates indicate that the fire, caused by a broken gas valve, did $250,000 worth of damage to the elevator and nearby offices.
4. The fire department and police cordoned off several blocks around the Wheeling Chemical Co. this morning after a fire damaged a section of the plant that uses chlorine gas.

WORKBOOK

A. IGNORANCE might interest the students. B. ACNE is more difficult; but it is on a subject that is obviously familiar to many of them.
     The final skill drill in this chapter, SKILL DRILL IV: AUDITING YOUR EMOTIONS, might prove interesting for you and your students.

EXERCISES

A.   Ignorance

Sr. Borges did visit the United States to lecture,
and he did speak to many college audiences. He is
elderly and when you use the exercise you may find
he has died. But plunge on, and assume all this is
recent. His quotes are accurate; McCarthy's are
invented. McCarthy and Mallory College are fictional.
    The story would be built around McCarthy's re-
actions to Sr. Borges' statement. Here is one approach:

        The chairman of the English Department
    of Mallory College said today he tends to
    agree with the comment of an Argentine writer
    that American college students are "extra-
    ordinarily ignorant."
        The South American author, Jorge Luis
    Borges, had toured the United States last
    year, visiting several campuses in this
    country, including Mallory. On his return
    to his country, Borges said:
        "American college students are...."
    His comments were recently published in
    a U.S. magazine.
        Prof. Justin McCarthy, who said his
    department was host to Borges during the
    writer's visit here, also was critical of
    students' knowledge of literature.
        "I've been teaching here and elsewhere
    ...." (Continue with McCarthy's quotes.)

    The students should be encouraged to put in any-
thing they can find on Sr. Borges from their references. Generally, you might remind them, critics
need to have their qualifications presented to readers so that their criticisms can be assessed against
their background.

B. Acne

This exercise has been used successfully for several years. Students enjoy doing it, perhaps because of their familiarity with the subject matter. It is also useful for instructors because it trains students to search such publications for good copy. The exercise also should help even the non-scientific student understand the scientific method.

One approach has been to talk the exercise through before the class has written a story. What are the necessities for the piece?

The source: title, date, authors, nature of publication.

Purpose of experiment.

How carried out.

Conclusion of study.

Style of authors. (This is often ignored by beginners. You might point out the good quotes that could be used: "holy furor...blacklisted items are delicious and delectable to the adolescent taste....")

Here is the beginning of one student's story:

> Teen-agers may once again gobble chocolate without fear or worry, say three skin specialists at the University of Pennsylvania in a report published this week.
>
> The skin disease acne - that bane of adolescents - is not aggravated by eating chocolate, the specialists say. Their study appears in the current issue of the "Journal of the American Medical Association."

It has been a truism among teen-agers that chocolate causes pimples. Most skin specialists have also believed this, the report states. But the authors - Drs. (name them) - say diet has little or nothing to do with acne.

Their experiment took two groups of.... (Describe experiment.)

Another lead:

For years adolescents with skin problems have been warned not to eat chocolate.

They can eat all they want, say three dermatologists from the University of Pennsylvania School of Medicine in Philadelphia.

The widely accepted theory that chocolate aggravates acne is false, they conclude in a study published in a current issue of the "Journal of the American Medical Association"....

Do not let a student write this without a little life to it. Make sure there are good quotes.

SKILL DRILL: AUDITING YOUR EMOTIONS

There are no right or wrong answers here. Journalists generally have neutral responses to emotional issues, or try to control their emotions when they are handling a story involving an individual or an organization that arouses strong feelings. A political conservative assigned to a union convention has to watch out for bias, as does a liberal handling a Republican meeting.

On the other hand, is it possible to be neutral about the Ku Klux Klan? Perhaps neutrality lies in absolute accuracy in observation and writing and in the careful elimination of inferences and judgments in copy.

You might want to use the answers for a survey of the class. You can do a class-wide analysis and then break down the answers into major groups, such as sex and race, if there are enough students in the class to justify the breakdowns.

6   PLANNING THE STORY

Chapter 6 offers two tracks for the student to follow in planning the story. There is the tried-and-true Five W's and an H and the more modern: Who said or did what? What happened?

You can take your pick in your instruction. In the real world, I've never heard a reporter mention the inverted pyramid or the Five W's and an H. Never in working in the east, southwest and far west have I heard the terms in a newsroom. And I rarely hear them these days from instructors. But use them if you believe they can be a helpful tool for beginners.

Editors are moving toward the delayed lead and informal story structure for news stories as well as for features. But for the beginner, the young man or woman who will be writing straight news stories on the first job, it would be best to drill the direct lead at this stage. Students want to write delayed leads, but for the wrong reason. Unable to find the lead to their stories, they often will write a de-layed lead in the hope the reader will do their work for them. Their delayed leads usually **are** what we call buried leads.

Once the student knows how to use the direct lead, the delayed lead can be tried.

The opening anecdote in this chapter, by the way, is about a well-known California editor, George Popo-vich. He was more bark than bite, but he could ter-rorize new staffers and make life unpleasant even for the old-timers. He was dedicated to making his news-paper the best, and so staffers did understand that it was not bile but pride that made him so demanding. You might want to try to instill pride of product in the students. After all, their names will be on the stories they write.

WORKBOOK

The exercises in this chapter of the workbook should
give students an opportunity to organize events with
several facts. As a starter, you could suggest that
students use a numbering system for the facts, assigning number 1 to the most important of the facts in the
material, 2 to the next most important and so on.
    For A. GOALS, students could do this in class.
You may well find that there is no agreement on No. 1.
It could be:

        • The call for an education that will de-
    velop a "free and open mind."

        • The need to teach students to spell and
    punctuate properly.

        • The quote from Whitehead that concludes
    the talk.

    As the students will see, there are no absolutes.
    In the following example, the news writer has
selected the "free and open mind" idea for the lead
and then immediately picked up spelling and punctuation.

EXERCISES

A. Goals

        A British literary critic last night
    told journalists and journalism educators
    that the aim of journalism education should
    be the development of a free and open mind.

Jeffrey St. George, the main speaker at
the annual state convention of the Daily Newspaper Association on the local college campus,
said journalism teachers must also meet the
needs of newspaper editors for reporters who
can spell and punctuate sentences correctly.

"Clearly, a professional education must
give the student skills and a sense of craft,"
he said in a speech prepared for delivery.

"But it is not enough to prepare the student only for his first job. The education
must be...."

Then go back to the "free and open mind" theme.

B. Wedding

This suit should be made into a feature. Still the
basics should be in the story: names and addresses
of the plaintiffs and of the defendants, basis for the
suit, amount of damages sought, where filed, the background of the incident. Make sure all assertions are
attributed to the plaintiffs. A possible start:

The first day of married life for Tobias
and Carolyn Lopez turned into a disaster for
them.

The Albuquerque newlyweds, who live at
712 Silver Ave., SW, assert in a suit in Ber-
nalillo County District Court today that they
had rented the Women's Club at 22 Gold Ave.,
SW, for a wedding celebration. But when the
couple and their 200 guests arrived, the club
was already occupied.

Another party with 100 guests was in
full swing....

In checking the student's stories, see whether they have followed the text's advice to rely on the S-V-O sentence structure. I'd say that 75 to 90 percent of most writers' sentences are in this form.

The textbook has five pictures at the beginning of the chapter with accompanying facts. The student is asked to decide whether he or she will write straight news stories or features. Here is my thinking about them:

1. WASHING-UP: The campus organization reports it collected $450 from its car wash service. This sounds like a straight news story. If the reporter were enterprising, he or she might have picked up some sidelights to make a feature story.
2. ROCK STAR: The interview with him by a staff reporter is filled with interesting anecdotes and incidents, which spells feature.
3. BURNOUT: Since two people were injured and lost their belongings, this is a straight news story.
4. COMING EVENT: This is a precede about the singer's appearance next month on campus. Since only the basic information is available now, this would be a straight news story, unless the reporter has sufficient background to write a feature.
5. STORM: The loss of this family's home to the sea is too serious to be anything but a straight news story.

This chapter can be taken up in the normal course of the term, or you may wish to use it for reference at any time. For example, during the first news writing exercises you may want to call the student's attention to the sections on accuracy and attribution.

Some instructors believe that the best way to teach students to write is to have them feel free of restrictions for the first few weeks, to allow them to write in a relaxed fashion. As they develop confidence, their writing may be made more disciplined by the use of such necessities as those included in this chapter.

Whichever route you decide to take, students should understand the ideas behind these rudiments. Perhaps one way to introduce students to these 10 elements is to ask them to clip examples of attribution, identification, balance and the like. They may even find poor examples, stories in which individuals have been inadequately identified or in which the victims of charges have not been allowed to have their say.

One of the criticisms of the current college student is that he or she is too accepting, too passive. For those students who want to try journalism as a career, passivity is no help. Encouraging students to be more critical users of the media will help to counter this tendency to accept.

WORKBOOK

SKILL DRILL: GUIDELINES will help the student apply several of the rudiments. If you consider some too difficult, you may want to indicate the general nature of the problem and ask the student to make the changes or corrections. For example, for A. SALARY, you might say the problem involves accuracy; for B. FINE, accuracy; C. RESIGNATION, attribution, and so on.

SKILL DRILL: GUIDELINES

A. Salary

Inaccurate. Students should be reminded to add or sub-
tract, as the case may be, when figures are given.
Here, the deductions total $53, which makes his take-
home pay $97; so the phrase should be "slightly under,"
not "more than."

B. Fine

Inaccurate. Loitering is a violation or a misdemeanor,
not a felony, in every city I know about. Tell students of the levels of offenses: violation, misdemean-
or, felony.

C. Resignation

Attribution problems. This is a common error among
beginners. The second sentence is made to appear as
fact, whereas it is Jenkins' opinion. Make it read:
He is quitting the force because of what he described
as (he asserted is)....

D. Shots

Brevity. The sentence seems to run on and on. One
solution:

        The city plans to round up unleashed dogs
    and fine their owners $15.
        Under a proposal by the city health de-
    partment, the dogs would also be given anti-
    rabies shots. They would be returned only
    after the fine is paid.

E. Success

Inaccurate. The Red Sox lost the Series to the Reds,
who are from Cincinnati (misspelled in the text).

F. Talk

Inaccurate. It is Mr. Lopez on second reference. In
Spanish, the mother's name usually is placed last and
the father's name after the person's given name. With
Spanish names, check the source.

G. Noise

The news point is buried. The lead is in the probable
demise of the housing proposal.

H. New Age

Attribution. For statements of this sort, we need to
know more about Goldman than the vague "a writer."
Writer of what? Where do his pieces appear?

I. Adoption

The news point is buried. Play up the human interest
angle: Dowle's heading the agency that placed him
for adoption in its first year of operation. You
might have the students try their hand at rewriting
this story.

J. Tour

Iceland is not the world's largest island; nor did
Eric the Red discover it. These facts apply to Green-
land, which may have been what the speaker said or
meant to say. In such cases, when the speaker cannot
be checked to verify the reporter's correction, the
change will be made or the item dropped.

The exercises in this chapter include features and straight news stories. I think students will have some fun with them. I hope that you can develop in your students the feeling that writing can be enjoyable. Finding the right lead, using quotes and anecdotes that fit the situation, and writing a well-organized story - these are creative acts that should give pleasure to students.

EXERCISES

A. Opening React

Students should focus on the complaints of the local merchants. They gave some excellent quotes. Here is a delayed lead:

> The student-run College Food Cooperative may have brought joy to the hearts and relief to the pocketbooks of students, but two local merchants are grim about the competition.
> Russell Rothkrug, owner of Russ's Market, criticized the college for subsidizing the students.
> "We have to operate at a profit, but these kids don't have families to support or rent to pay. I think it's unfair," Rothkrug said.
> He said his business has dropped 20 percent since the campus store opened 10 days ago.
> Another merchant,...

B. Cab

In the workbook, the McHughs are from Brigantine, N.J.

Newlyweds Find
New York's No Honeymoon

By Bruce Drake

The cabby, to the great surprise of newlyweds Ronald and Marie McHugh of Carbondale, Pa., didn't wait around for a tip. Or, for that matter, to be paid. Unfortunately, neither did he pause to unload their luggage before roaring off on Park Avenue.

That's how the McHughs' intended weeklong honeymoon at the Waldorf-Astoria began Saturday. They had known New York City was no bed of roses, but this was ridiculous. And with that taste of the Big Apple, the McHughs decided yesterday that their new marriage would be better celebrated back home in Carbondale.

"We were going to see some shows and then see Guy Lombardo on New Year's Eve," said Mrs. McHugh ruefully. "This has got to be the shortest honeymoon in history."

Here is McHugh's version of what happened:

The couple, in their 50s, were married Friday night in Scranton, Pa., and on Saturday arrived in the city by bus. They hailed a cab outside the Port Authority terminal and directed the driver to the Waldorf.

"Ronald got out, with the money for the driver in his hand, and waited by the back of the cab for the driver to come out and open the trunk," Mrs. McHugh said. "Then the doorman helped me out of the car ...and all of a sudden - I couldn't believe my eyes - the cab just zoomed off."

In the cab's trunk, she said, was a cosmetic bag and three pieces of luggage. Inside the luggage, along with the couple's clothes, were some wedding gifts including two envelopes with $100 in each.

The McHughs hopped in another cab, at the doorman's suggestion, and attemped to follow the original taxi. But that cops-and-robbers tactic failed. "The first cab

43

just had all the lights in his favor and we lost him after five blocks," Mrs. McHugh said.

The couple, however, had noted the cab's license plate and reported it to police of the Midtown North station. Police tracked the cab down to a Queens-based fleet but recovered only one suitcase, which Mrs. McHugh said had been "ransacked."

The suitcase, said Detective Michael Hanley, was found in the back seat of the cab by a driver on a later shift. He said the driver who allegedly made off with the McHugh's luggage was still being sought for questioning.

"All I know is that if they get the guy who did this I will most certainly come back and press charges," vowed Mrs. McHugh. "You might say I'm really teed about this."

-<u>Daily News</u>

C. Waiter

Unlike the experience of the couple from Brigantine, here is something good about that den of iniquity, New York City. This may be worth a few paragraphs. This, too, is a true story.

Here is the beginning of a story done by a student, which is just as good as the piece the reporter who handled the story wrote. The student used her imagination for this delayed lead:

Money goes fast these days. But for Mrs. Arthur Katzen of 896 Armour Blvd. it seemed to evaporate in her purse on a recent trip to New York.

The immediate reaction of most people who associate missing money with New York is thievery, a quick-fingered pickpocket perhaps. But let Mrs. Katzen tell the story:
(Pickup the quotes from the exercise.)

D. Stuck

Another actual situation. Any bright but not silly
lead will do. Make sure that the students do not poke
fun at Mrs. Wright. Although no libel would be involved since this is a legal action and privileged,
it would be unfair to use her for laughs.

> A suit in Civil Court had a happy ending
> today for Beulah Wright of 87 West End Ave.
> A jury awarded her $4,300 in damages be-
> cause of an incident on an Intercity Bus Co.
> bus in August....

E. No Baby

Again, a bright is called for, but make sure the students do not give the elephant human characteristics.

> No, Baby isn't expecting.
> Five months ago, hopes were raised that
> the African elephant might be pregnant.
> But the latest word from the local zoo
> is: "False pregnancy."

F. Hot Line

This exercise has been the subject of some debate.
Obviously, there is some humor in the event (which
occurred, if memory serves me right, during Eisen-
hower's presidency). But, ask the serious-minded,
how can you poke fun at such a potentially serious
subject?
The serious story:

> The president's office today confirmed
> a report that the president had been awakened
> recently by a wrong-number call on the hot
> line which is used by the Pentagon to inform
> him of an enemy attack.

45

The caller had wanted the animal shelter, the president's press secretary reported. The following conversation took place:...

A delayed lead could be used on a humorous story:

One night recently the president's hot line rang.

This is the closely guarded telephone link between the Pentagon and the White House to be used to inform the president of an enemy attack. It would carry his reply that could unleash nuclear war.

But this was no practice ring. The caller was in earnest.

"Is this the animal hospital?" the caller asked....

Students usually find writing good leads to be their greatest challenge. Some instructors believe news story structure is the more troublesome for beginners. As I try to make clear at the beginning of the chapter, once the lead is decided on, the structure seems to take care of itself.

At the outset, emphasize the thinking and planning that go into lead writing. Have students follow the four steps outlined in the chapter, the first one being: What do I want to say? It's worth spending a lot of time on this concept. News writers talk to themselves as they write. Persuade your students to hold a dialogue with themselves as they plan their leads. They should always be asking themselves: What really happened here? What is it I am trying to say in this story? How can I reduce it to a subject and a verb?

Do not worry about the length of leads for now. The emphasis should be on finding the right lead for the story, no matter how long. If the theme is found and the lead happens to run on, it's not hard to cut.

Anyway, as I say in the text, some long leads are perfectly acceptable. Look at this one by Bill Serrin of The New York Times, written about the death of the first woman who had died mining coal:

What he could not forget, after he had left the hospital where she lay, still in her sweatshirt and long underwear and coveralls, on an emergency room cart, was that there was nothing to suggest she was dead.

A good lead is a good lead. The short lead usually is easier to understand than the long lead. But some subjects - like death in this <u>Times</u> lead - seem to call for a somberness that length emphasizes.

WORKBOOK

For practice in lead writing, you can try the unused material in any of the prior workbook exercises. I recommend trying any of the stories students did not use in chapter 1, DEVELOPING THE STORY IDEA and FINDING THE THEME. From chapter 2, try FINDING THE THEME.

You should take the students through the four steps:

1. What do I want to say? What is the theme?
2. Is this a straight news story or a feature?
3. Do I use a direct or a delayed lead?
4. What do I put into the lead?

Then have the students write the leads.

For additional practice in step 3, SKILL DRILL I: LEAD CHOICE.

For practice in tightening leads, try SKILL DRILL II: SIMPLIFYING.

SKILL DRILL I: LEAD CHOICE

These are not, the students should be told, absolute answers. Here are my suggestions:

A. Direct.
B. Either. (A delayed lead could be well done if the student knows Gilbert and Sullivan.)
C. Either, depending upon the local situation. If the issue has been discussed at length, then this story should have a direct lead.
D. Direct.
E. Direct. (Unless the subject matter lends itself to a delayed lead.)

F. Delayed.
G. Either.
H. Either.
I. Direct.
J. Either. (If this is a formal piece, direct would
   be best.)
K. Direct.
L. Direct.
M. Either, though I would lean to a direct lead be-
   cause of the seriousness of the matter.
N. Direct. (No one can play around with this kind
   of story.)
O. Either.

SKILL DRILL II: SIMPLIFYING

There are, of course, many ways to handle these leads.
Here are my suggestions, mixed with those I have had
from students who have done this drill:

A. The city will spend a total of $118,000 repairing
   three city streets this summer.
B. Police arrested 19-year-old Eileen McGuire in a
   Chicago bus depot today and charged her with arson in the $2-million Karvette Department Store
   fire.
C. Bids will be opened Dec. 10 for an all-electronic
   newsroom at the State University School of Journalism that will enable students to write and edit
   news without typewriters or pencils.
D. Connie Hawkins, the Bullets' newly acquired for-
   ward, led his new teammates to an 88-87 come-from-
   behind win over the Warriors.
E. Norris Josephson yesterday was sentenced to a
   minimum of five years in the state penitentiary
   for defrauding local residents of more than
   $500,000.
F. No relief is in sight next week for corn and
   wheat growers in drought-stricken Minnesota.

G. F.W. Walkenhorst, a university regent, today predicted the state legislature will not approve the university budget unless the faculty takes on a heavier course load.
H. (This lead needs little improvement if any. I would let it stand or perhaps inject the word "causing" before "millions of dollars in destruction.")
I. A Washington political reporter said last night that the modern advertising techniques used by politicians have made the political reporter unnecessary.
J. A national organization today filed suit in federal court against the U.S. Commission on Education, charging the federal agency with violating the separation of church and state by assigning public school teachers to religious schools.

You may want to ask the students to answer the questions asked in the outline over the pictures at the beginning of the chapter. The questions refer to the first three steps of the "Four Steps to the Lead." You can take the student through the fourth step if you provide additional information in class.
Here are my suggestions for the answers:

BLAZE: A WHAT theme. Straight news story. Direct lead.

OFFICIAL: A WHO lead. Straight news story. Direct lead.

SHARK: A WHAT lead. Straight news story. Direct lead. (If the reporter gathered some quotes from the fisherman who landed the big shark in the picture, this could be a feature story with a delayed lead.)

ROCK: A WHO lead: This can be a straight news story with a direct lead or a feature story with a delayed lead, depending on the approach.

SPRING: A WHAT lead. Feature story with a delayed lead. (See weather stories in chapter 15 of the textbook.)

This may be one of the most difficult chapters in the
textbook for the student. I suggest that you tell
students to use it as a reference, to be consulted
when they have trouble organizing long stories. Or
you can spend one class session on these concepts.
    Story organization is a major problem for begin-
ning journalists. There is not much problem organizing a single-element story. But many stories reporters are now called upon to write are complex, and
editors are wary of the one-element story. Newspapers want their reporters to dig, to give the full
dimension of the event, which often involves the
reporter in more than one theme.
    The key to story structure is the linear frame-
work--the elements in the lead taken in order and
amplified.

WORKBOOK

I suggest you start students off by looking over
actual straight news stories - if they are well written. DISCUSSION: ANALYSIS gives students directions
for analyzing a story. Start with single-element
stories, such as A. BIDS and any they find in their
local newspaper. You then may go on to two-element
stories and then to three-element stories.
    For multiple-element stories, ask students to
analyze the lead to see which of the options the
writer used: (1) the lead with all elements in one
sentence; (2) the lead with one sentence per element;
or (3) the summary lead.
    Exercises II includes a number of events that
have more than a single element.

EXERCISE I

A. Bids

This story is well organized, with the lead emphasiz-
ing the bids on renovation of the Scott building.
Here is a paragraph breakdown:

Lead - A: Renovation bids
2nd pgh.: Background to event
3rd pgh.: Amplification of lead - A_1
4th pgh.: Introduction of secondary material
      B: Police vehicles
      C: Pickup trucks
      D: Paving of Elm
5th pgh.: Amplification of lead - A_2
6th pgh.: Amplification of B - B_1
7th pgh.: Amplification of C - C_1
8th pgh.: Amplification of D - D_1
9th pgh.: Additional material
      E: Fireproofing building

EXERCISES II

A. Bus

This is a standard press release. The student should
be encouraged to scrutinize the release for an interesting aspect of the event the press officer has not
emphasized. The fact that the service would cater
mostly to domestic workers could be the basis of a
lead, which might be:

> The People's Bus Line, of 1320 East Tor-
> rence Ave., today asked the state Public
> Utilities Commission for permission to oper-
> ate a bus service that would take domestic
> workers from outlying communities into town.

Or:

Local domestic workers may find their commuting troubles solved if the state Public Utilities Commission grants a local man permission to operate a bus line into town.

B. Missing

There are a number of ideas in this story, a few of which could be made into a lead. There are two basic elements: the child's being located, and the admission of the babysitter that she had left the child at a friend's home. This could be the basic structure of the story.

> Billy Joe Appel, 4, of 801 Second Ave., was found this afternoon at the home of a friend of the child's babysitter, 15 hours after he had been reported missing by the babysitter last night.
> The babysitter, Alice Kragler, admitted under questioning by the police that she had taken the child to the home of the friend, Mrs. Bernice McCoy, at 320 Manley St. last night at 9 o'clock. The child is the son of Mr. and Mrs. Alan Appel.
> Police said she told them she wanted "to get even with the Appels for not letting me have my boyfriend visit me when I was baby-sitting with Billy Joe." She had told the Appels their son wandered off when she fell asleep looking at television.
> Miss Kragler said she had asked Mrs. McCoy to care for the child because she had been called home, the police said. When Mrs. McCoy heard on the radio that the child had been reported missing she was too frightened to act, the police said.
> The Appels said they would not press charges against Miss Kragler.

"Alice is a good girl," Mrs. Appel said. "She just got upset. She loves Billy Joe and would never let anything happen to him."

The police said a report of the incident will be turned over to juvenile authorities.

About 20 volunteers searched the woods near the Appel home last night after the child's disappearance.

C. Calendar

Students may be tempted to write a summary lead, but the importance of Senator Kennedy is such that his scheduled speech should be the lead. The other events can be listed by date and summarized.

D. Daredevil

This accident lends itself to a delayed lead:

Alan Taylor may not have as many lives as a cat, but fate had three chances to claim him last night, and he survived them all.

The state highway patrol reports that Taylor, 20, was driving on an overpass over the Amtrak tracks 20 miles east of Canton when he apparently lost control of the vehicle.

The car broke through a guardrail, struck a power line in its descent, and landed on the tracks upside down. Taylor, a short-order cook, was trapped inside his car for 15 minutes. When he was freed, he walked away, unhurt.

A few minutes before the accident, the eastbound Broadway Limited passed over the tracks.

But Taylor has a few things to worry
about - he was cited for reckless and drunk-
en driving, driving without a license and
speeding.

Watch out for students who like to call on the
miraculous for Taylor's survival. Miracles are performed in Lourdes, not on Amtrak tracks.

E. Outage

Some 50 homes in Arden Hills were without power this afternoon for 38 minutes after
an automobile struck a power pole at 1 p.m....

F. Lifesaver

The story should begin with information about the
local showing of the film and follow with a brief
description of the procedure to aid choking victims.
The story should not try to be the authoritative
guide to this procedure.

G. Picket

Obviously, the local is angry, but the state office
knows the reality of politics and probably will not
revoke its endorsement. The student should not, of
course, say this in the copy, but neither should the
student overemphasize the possibility of revocation
of the endorsement. Here is one way to approach the
event:

A Freeport labor union charged Alex-
ander Spivak, the Democratic candidate for
the Senate, with "subterfuge" in entering
the struck Belmont Motel this noon by a back
door to avoid a picket line at the entrance.

The Hotel and Restaurant Employees union said it has asked the state office of the parent union, the AFL-CIO, to reconsider its endorsement of Spivak. In response, the state office scheduled a meeting for 8 p.m. Friday in Freeport with the local.

The incident began when Spivak, who was to address a luncheon meeting of the local Lions Club, noticed the picket line in front of the motel. His press aide said that Spivak had not known of the strike and would not cross the picket line.

"So we went in the back," his aide said.

Bert Gentle, state director of the AFL-CIO, said that revocations of an endorsement are rare. He could recall only one. There have been occasional censures, he added.

The statement issued by Spivak has not been used because of its irrelevancy to the event and its self-serving nature. This might be worth discussing.

A reminder: The textbook seems to make the news story structure mechanistic. You may not want to be as rigid in your approach as the textbook. Obviously, writers break the rules all the time, and their stories are gems. But good writers know the rules and are able to move beyond them. My approach is to have students learn the rules and to build on them so that they can fly free when it is time for them to soar.

An anecdote for your class: James Reston of The New York Times is supposed to have advised a young reporter who asked him how to put a story together: "Write your stories in the shape of a Q. Start off with something interesting, like an anecdote or description that ties in with the story. Write all the way around the subject. When you come back to the beginning, give it a twist."

I have tried to make students conscious of the proper
use of language by listing at the beginning of the
chapter some blunders and bloopers I have seen around
the country. I assure you that every one of these is
authentic. You might ask students to start a collec-
tion of their own, or to take a few examples to class.

Since words are going to be their close associ-
ates, for this term at least, students may as well
make words their friends. It seems to me that many
students have trouble writing because they approach
words with fear or resentment.

One home assignment might help. Have students
collect examples in these categories:

> Bad grammar
>
> Misspellings
>
> Incorrect punctuation
>
> Misused words
>
> Redundancies
>
> Clichés
>
> Mixed metaphors

They can spot these in textbooks, student papers,
signs, brochures and advertisements as well as in
newspapers. Here is the page one headline of The
Tampa Tribune, March 22, 1982:

> Hoards Gather for Shuttle Flight 3

The next day, the paper told readers, "Hordes of editors are now poring over the Tribune's horde of
dictionaries.

WORKBOOK

The skill drills on grammar, punctuation and spelling
may be used early in the term. You may find that
your students are weak on these fundamentals and must
be drilled before they are able to move ahead on news
writing.

SKILL DRILL I: SPELLING

The 50 words most frequently misspelled have been
taken from several college grammar books and from my
own experience. If there is a hierarchy of misspell-
ings, numbers 12, 19, 21-27 and 29 would top the list.
It might be interesting to see what percentage of the
words that are checkmarked (meaning students would
have consulted the dictionary) are misspelled. Perhaps words that the students thought they knew are
misspelled just as often.

Answers

1a.	8a.	15b.	21b.	27a.	33b.	39b.	45b.
2a.	9b.	16b.	22a.	28b.	34b.	40b.	46a.
3a.	10a.	17b.	23b.	29a.	35b.	41a.	47a.
4a.	11a.	18b.	24a.	30b.	36b.	42b.	48b.
5a.	12b.	19a.	25a.	31a.	37a.	43a.	49a.
6b.	13a.	20b.	26a.	32b.	38b.	44a.	50a.
7a.	14a.						

The chronic bad spellers should be required to
carry a pocket dictionary. Those of you with the
strength to give spelling drills, more power to you.
There are plenty of lists available. My last resort
is to return--unread--papers with several spelling
errors. When I hit the third error, I stop reading,
return the paper and give the student overnight to
clear up the blunders.

SKILL DRILL II: GRAMMAR, PUNCTUATION AND STYLE

Grammar

   A. This is such an egregious error it might stick
in the minds of students who have a tendency to
dangle modifiers. If it does not work, try
item L in this list.
   B. Comma splice. Make into two sentences.
   C. <u>Its</u>, not it's.
D.&E. Second sentences are not sentences. Replace
periods with commas.
   F. Make it <u>all</u> <u>right</u>.
   G. The second sentence is not a sentence. Replace
period with a comma or put the phrase at the
beginning of the sentence with a comma between
the two.
   H. The second sentence is not a sentence. Replace
period with comma.
   I. <u>It's</u> instead of its.
   J. Everyone is singular: Everyone hoped <u>he</u> or
<u>she</u> could help.
   K. Team is singular. The team played as though it
wanted to win.
   L. Dangling modifier.

Punctuation

One of the best descriptions of punctuation I have
seen is this: Punctuation is visual inflection.
    The purpose of punctuation is to clarify meaning.
The comma is used to mark a short pause and thus will
separate material that might be difficult to grasp if
it runs together. The period is a full stop.

A. The two men, each of whom had a hat pulled over
    his eyes, entered the store.
B. To confuse them, the owner busied himself at the
    rear.
C. He asked, "What do you want?"
D. "Nothing," the taller one answered.
E. The children's, men's and women's departments lost
    money last year.
F. He took James's books and ran. (The rule is that
    one syllable words ending in an <u>s</u> add <u>'s.</u>)
G. He asked whose book it is.
H. "Why do you want to know?" he asked.
I. The question--which was shot out like a bullet--
    left him dazed. (Or two commas in place of the
    dashes can be used.)
J. He enjoyed daydreaming, but some people thought
    him a little loony. (The quotation mark should
    be used when quoting someone.)

Style, Word Usage

A. <u>Principle</u> instead of principal.
B. <u>Elusive</u> instead of illusive.
C. <u>Complimented</u> instead of complemented.
D. <u>Loose</u>, not lose.
E. <u>Stationery</u>, not stationary.
F. <u>Hoard</u>, not horde (although to beginners it may
    seem this way).
G. <u>Dominate</u>, not domineer.
H. This sentence violates parallel structure: Mil-
    ton's percentage of...Shakespeare's percentage
    of...and the King James Bible's percentage of....
    Or: The percentage of Anglo-Saxon words in Mil-
    ton was 81, in Shakespeare 90 and in the King
    James Bible 94.
I. <u>Consult</u>, not consultate.
J. <u>Avoid</u>, not avert.
K. <u>Advice</u>, not advise; <u>affects</u>, not effects.
L. Media and criteria are plural; follow both with
    <u>are</u>, not is.
M. <u>Fewer</u>, not less.

N. <u>Infer</u>, not imply. (If the writer is referring to the readers who suggest to others that poor writing is the case, <u>imply</u> is correct.)
O. <u>Ever</u>, not never. <u>As</u>, not like.
P. True is unnecessary, redundant.
Q. Eliminate discursively and wordy or verbose. Redundant.
R. <u>Expect</u>, not anticipate. Delete <u>literally</u>.
S. <u>Then</u>, for at that point in time.
T. <u>Now</u>, for at this point in time.
U. A contradiction. All facts are true. Rewrite. (If the sentence is a direct quote, then it can be used, of course.)
V. <u>Persuaded</u> for convinced.
W. <u>Concrete</u> for cement. Cement is a powder and is one of the ingredients in making concrete and concrete blocks.
X. Collision or a similar word for mishap, which describes a minor accident.
Y. <u>It's</u> for its.

SKILL DRILL III: ABUSED AND MISUSED WORDS

Some of these words have been abused in SKILL DRILL I. This should put the student's knowledge to work.

EXERCISE

EXERCISE A. SYRACUSE is fun for students. Give an award to the student who spots the most cliches and trite expressions.

A. Syracuse

As the well-informed football follower in your class will no doubt point out, this goes back many a year. Ernie Davis was a Syracuse player, and a fine one, more than 15 years ago. The sportswriting jargon is classical in its magnificent use of cliches and I am including it as Horrible Example No. 1 for any budding sportswriters in your class. I found seven cliches or trite expressions, but one student insisted he had found 10. As I recall he proved it to me. I do know the third paragraph has three. He added a fourth ("fleet 6-2, 205-pound speedster") to my three: "world beater...As the expression goes... all the tools."

Toward the end of the chapter 10 pictures are shown under the heading, "The Right Word." Have the students select one word or two that describes what is shown. Here are some suggestions:

Crowd: A basketball game. But whether this is the exhilaration of VICTORY or the students are furious because of the referee's call and are shouting ROBBED, is unclear. Either word will do.

Pumpkins: I like pumpkin pie, so I would say YUMMY. Maybe it's heavy, and the emotion is WHEW.

Basketball: The sports fans may say LAYUP. Others may make it AIRBORNE.

Horses: This serene scene could be HOME-BOUND.

Women: This looks like some kind of REUNION. Maybe it's a sorority RUSH. Or just plain JOY.

Athlete: Looks like the starting line for a race: GET READY.

As for writing leads, anything goes so long as the students use the word or words they have selected to describe the scene.

Here are a batch of boners that press association reporters made. You may want to use them in a lecture, or you may want to give them to students as a test at the end of their work on language essentials. If students spot half the errors, they are doing well:

62

1. BEIRUT, Iraq - Fighting intensified around Abadan Saturday....
2. ...embankment located near Stockton about 40 miles west of San Francisco....
3. NEW YORK - The temperature plunged to zero degrees today.
4. OMAHA, Neb. - Firefighters today conquered a raging explosion-triggered blaze at a grain elevator....
5. CLEVELAND - A British mother of five, the chief weapon in a battle to save the 10-month-old victim of an often fatal bone disease....
6. ...have tried to diffuse the potentially volatile situation.
7. His apartment was robbed two days before Christmas while....
8. The London Ripper is generally accredited with....
9. PEKING - China celebrated May Day in relaxed but muted....
10. Thousands of parade-crazed New Yorkers crammed the curbs....
11. He looks like a poet....
12. SYDNEY, Australia - Albert Henry, the disposed former premier of the Cook Islands, has died in....
13. Less lightning deaths were recorded last year....
14. NEW YORK - A report prepared for the city bar association refuted the claims that....
15. PORT JEFFERSON, N.Y. - The Coast Guard said the clean-up will take a couple more days.

The Errors

1. Beirut is the capital of Lebanon. It's not in Iraq.
2. The location of Stockton would put it deep in the Pacific. The writer meant east, not west.
3. Zero degrees is like having your wallet stuffed with no cash. Zero is just zero.
4. When the fat on a stove ignites briefly, that's a blaze. When there is a raging fire, it's hardly a blaze. This is a matter of word usage.

5. How can a woman be a weapon? Again, word usage.
6. Words that sound alike are sometimes confused by writers. The proper word is defused.
7. Confusion between robbery and burglary. A person is robbed, a place is burglarized.
8. A school is accredited. People are credited with something.
9. The word but is often used instead of "and." That's wrong. But introduces a contrast to what has preceded it. The writer meant relaxed and muted.
10. New Yorkers are a strange lot. But parade crazed? The writer is trying too hard.
11. We tend to stereotype jobs, professions, vocations. Just what does a poet look like? Two of the most successful twentieth-century American poets were an insurance executive and a physician.
12. The writer meant deposed.
13. Not less. The word is fewer.
14. To refute means to disprove. Since reporters rarely know whether the source actually disproved claims, use the verb to rebut.
15. It's a couple of more days.

One way to drive home the point about short sentences
and everyday language is to have students clip a
story or column by a news writer they like. If you
wish, they can even copy a few paragraphs of a favorite author. Have the students try to diagnose their
choices by beginning with average sentence length.
Then ask the students to circle any word with which
they are unfamiliar.
    They are bound to discover the virtues of short
sentences and ordinary language.
    Also, you might have them apply the readability
formula to various publications. They can compare
Time, Reader's Digest and Atlantic, or any magazines
you chose. You might give them the circulation of
some magazines. I'll wager that circulation is in-
versely proportional to sentence length: The Digest's
sentences should average 10-15 words, whereas The
Nation, The New Republic, Atlantic or Harper's will
have sentences averaging 20-plus words. But don't
suggest that such magazines are useless. Their readers do not find 20-word sentences difficult. It's
like comparing Faulkner and Hemingway. Each has his
virtues.
    Suggest that the cause of unclear writing is
thinking. Remind students that muddy thinking equals
muddy writing. One tactic some instructors use is to
ask students to write a headline for their story before writing it. This seems to clear the mind of
clutter.
    I have included two fairly long examples of good
writing style in the section headed "Natural Style."
One is about a fire that took five lives and the
other is about life in a housing project. You might
want to study these examples with the class.

65

If you can develop students who write clearly and convincingly, then you are doing very well indeed. Having students write with some grace and with a style that can be fitted to the events they write about is a bonus. I would emphasize clarity. Then conviction.

To make the point about the importance of writing convincingly, you might ask students to bring to class stories they found convincing and those they did not. See whether you can establish guidelines from the samples.

The anecdote that begins the section on convincing writing was supplied by a former student who was reporting from Central America. The story he wrote about restlessness among the people was convincing because of the human interest anecdotes and quotes he used. (The stories of this kind may have convinced readers, but they failed to convince the U.S. government, which continued to support the dictator until the people finally rebelled, tossed him out and formed a revolutionary government.)

The idea of having students clip stories they like could be used to make many points about fine writing. For a home assignment, students could be instructed to list the reasons they liked one or two stories. Have them take their clippings and reasons to class and try to reach some agreement in the class about the principles of good writing.

WORKBOOK

DISCUSSION: A. READABLE is useful as a home assignment. EXERCISE A. ARTFUL could be fun. B. COACH is a little more difficult but may not be beyond your students' ability to handle with some flashes of style.

EXERCISES

A. Artful

The story below looks like the handiwork of Bob Peck,
one of the great rewrite men on the staff of the old
New York Herald Tribune, which was known as a writer's
newspaper.

A tall, slim and elusive twenty-eight-year-old named Arthur Howard left Brooklyn Felony Court a free (but wanted) man yesterday by the simple expedient of walking out, much to the embarrassment of all concerned.

Howard, who gave his address as 585 Throop Ave., Brooklyn, was in court to answer a charge of snatching a woman's pocketbook. He told Magistrate Harry Serper he wanted the court to assign him a lawyer, and was asked to sit down and wait.

He sat down, but he didn't wait. When Magistrate Serper called the case, Arthur Howard wasn't there. He had, it appeared, slipped calmly out, threading his way apologetically through a small crowd of police, court attendants and prisoners.

You might want to point to the "voice" of the
Herald Tribune piece. Events have a way of requiring
the voice or style in which the piece should be written. Because of the way Howard left the courtroom--
quietly, unobtrusively, almost leisurely--the story
was written with longer-than-usual sentences in a calm,
peaceful style. Had Howard shot his way to freedom,
the voice would have been sharp, abrupt, staccato.

Norman Podhoretz, the editor of Commentary magazine, says that writing requires the writer to find
"the magical key," which he describes as "the tone of
voice, the only tone of voice in which this particular
piece of writing will permit itself to be written. To
find that tone is to unlock the floodgates."

67

B. Coach

Here is how the piece appeared in the Clear Creek Courant, under the byline of Patricia Rounds. It could appear in this form in the Denver newspaper--with a dateline--for which the students are supposed to write.

Ten-year-old Joe Pretz and 13 other would-be Georgetown Red Sox have everything going for them.

They've got energy and enthusiasm.

They've got numbers.

They have the will to play baseball and to practice and play the game well.

But they don't have a coach.

And if they don't have a coach, they can't play in the Little League when games start June 14.

Regardless, the 8- to 11-year-old baseball players practice whenever they can manage it.

But in the meantime they've been busy trying to muster up a coach to work with them.

Apparently, everyone they've asked is tied up, or tied down. Regardless, no one has the time to do it, so far.

In an interview with the Clear Creek Courant, Joe Pretz was asked what he thought was the best reason why someone should want to coach his team.

"Because we need a coach," he said simply.

Pretz's friend, Bill Geiger, decided to help by putting a classified ad in the Courant: "Wanted Right Away - Baseball Coach."

Geiger said he offered to pay for the ad because the boys "are in the same pickle as Charlie Brown, you know."

"But there's no girls or beagles on the team," he added.

Stacy Bartels wants to play, too, along with....

I have tried to give students some idea of the work
life of a television anchor person so that they understand that broadcast journalism requires the same
dedication, labor and knowledge that print journalism
demands. You might invite some local broadcast journalists to chat with the class about their work.
Some stations welcome visitors to view newscasts from
the studio.
 For writing practice, use the AP or UPI wire,
not the radio wire. If your department does not sub-
scribe to this service, then you might clip news stories for the class. You might also make an arrange-
ment with a local radio or television station to
obtain its news scripts. You could then show students
the newspaper version and the rewritten broadcast
copy.

WORKBOOK

For any of the exercises, and for those that you may
design, try to have the students first derive the
major theme from the wire or newspaper copy. This
should help them to reduce the news copy to manage-
able size.
 Next, have them write the lead based on the
theme. If the theme is complicated, suggest an introduction, a background or a headline-type sentence.
 Before they turn in their copy, ask students to
check sentence length - no sentence over 25 words,
average sentence length about 15 words.
 The workbook has four exercises that you might
try, although I think the best practice might be to
take local stories from the newspaper and have the
class work on them.

EXERCISES

A. Solitary

Forgetting books for class can land
a Michigan youngster in solitary confinement. So can talking out of turn or walking around the classroom without permission.
After four such incidents, the youngster is
sent off to a room nine by twelve or six by
nine. Although parents had the rule
scrapped last month, the Carrollton District school board has reinstated it by a
hefty majority--six to one. No bread and
water for the youngsters, though. Lunch is
brought in and they are allowed two rest-
room breaks during their six-and-a-half
hour confinement.

B. Hoofer

It takes two to tangle. And it took
a fire rescue unit to untie the two in downtown New York City. A taxi and a horse
pulling a hansom cab tried to negotiate the
same corner. The taxi won, but the horse
had the last laugh. It caught its right
front hoof in the rear bumper of the taxi,
and the two had to wait until the fire squad
untangled them.

C. Lakes

Orlando's growth is killing its once-crystal-clear lakes. The eighty-two lakes that give the central Florida city its picture card look are dying. Victims of pollution. This is the grim analysis of a consulting firm, Mills and Precourt. The consultants say the water that drains from Orlando's rooftops, driveways, parking lots and streets is so polluted the lakes may die. The consultants say the only solution is spending millions of dollars and adopting strict anti-pollution and drainage laws.

D. Nukerock

The muse is going to the aid of the anti-nuclear movement. An organization of popular musicians called Musicians United for Safe Energy--that's MUSE--will give two benefit concerts in New York in September to raise a million dollars for safe-energy technologies. MUSE members who will perform include James Taylor, the Doobie Brothers and Jackson Browne.

13   SPOT NEWS INTERVIEWS AND PROFILES

Some students have a hard time understanding the difference between the spot news interview, in which the event is the theme of the story, and the profile, in which the individual being interviewed is the focus of the story.

WORKBOOK

One way to make the difference clear is to look at some of the exercises in the workbook. In chapter 7, A. OPENING REACT and D. STUCK can be used to illustrate the spot news interview.

A.   The theme is the competition the student grocery poses to local merchants.
D.   The theme is the situation. If the person involved had been the mayor or someone of equal prominence, then the emphasis would have been on the who, not the what happened.

More ambitious spot news interviews are offered in this chapter in the workbook: A. FLIES and B. SUSPENSION.

For the profile, C. GALLOWAY and D. CRITICISM might interest students. They both involve journalism. Their comments could be the basis of a class discussion, which you might enjoy even if you do not use the exercises for writing work.

NOTE: For an exercise in having the students understand the idea of the nonnegotiable necessities of the story, try the SKILL DRILL: NECESSITIES. You can be specific about some of these, naming, for example, a local building that burned down in D. BLAZE or the local couple divorcing in M. SPLIT, and so on.

EXERCISES

A. Flies

This exercise lends itself to an anecdotal or a delayed lead. Not many of the exercises have stressed this kind of lead, the assumption being that students should first master the direct lead. The experiment with the wasp could be used, or the litany of pollutants in the last paragraph might start off the piece:

> The ever-present and pesky fly may someday disappear from the farm.
> The fly-destroyer is not an insecticide but another insect, the parasitic wasp. The use of the wasp was described by....

Or:

> Sewage in the oceans. Chemicals in the rivers. Asphalt spread over the farmland. Deadly fumes in the air we breathe.
> "Disaster on the horizon," said Roger Alexander, a biochemist in town to talk to the state chapter of the Friends of Nature....

In this kind of story, the best procedure is to
quote the source and to use an occasional paragraph
about the source that does not impede the flow of the
narrative. The student might be encouraged to insert any recent or local information, such as new
findings about mercury in water and in fish and the
like.

B. Suspension

A summary lead followed by a detailed list of rights
and grounds for suspension is one approach:

>   The city schools system today announced
> a new disciplinary code for students that
> grants them increased rights.
>   The code, announced by Herbert Gilkey-
> son, the city schools superintendent, gives
> students summoned for a disciplinary hearing
> these rights:

>   Presence of an attorney at the hearing.
>   An appeal within the school of the de-
> cision at the hearing.
>   An appeal beyond the school to the
> courts.

>   The new code follows a decision of the
> Supreme Court of the United States that ex-
> tends the constitutional rights of students....

A lead that is more specific:

>   Students in the city schools who face
> disciplinary action may take attorneys to
> their hearings and are entitled to appeal
> the decisions.
>   These rights were included in a new stu-
> dent disciplinary code announced today by....

C. Galloway

This is a picture of the ideal reporter. I think
they can get a sense of the man from these quotes,
and perhaps a sense of the journalist's mission,
too. These comments, it seems to me, strike closer
to the heart of the morality of journalism than all
the lectures about free lunches and free press-box
seats at ball games.
      There are several good quotes in here - no rou-
tine stories, only stories covered routinely; you
write of real people, and you owe them their reality;
a good reporter is a student all his life; read for
your life. I would not tell you which one to emphasize, but I would suggest that students use the little
story he tells about his friend in Texas. The paper
is in Victoria.

D. Criticism

This is an invented personality, although most of the
quotes are taken from the ruminations of a veteran
reporter for The Los Angeles Times that ran in Editor
& Publisher several years ago. Why do the old-timers
always think the world or their profession is going
to pot? Despite that tendency, Cole does have some
valid points. A lead might emphasize his poor opinion of young reporters. Make sure the student blends
Cole's personality and his background into the piece.

      A veteran reporter and editor has some
advice for schools of journalism now beset
by record numbers of students:
      "If they can't write or spell, counsel
them - or flunk them out."
      Frederick Cole, a retired editor of news-
papers in Florida, California and Michigan
who is here to advise the local newspapers on
changes in coverage and makeup, says too many
incompetents are trying to become reporters.
      "Too many applicants lack...."

Go on and quote this long section at length, interspersing the quotes with some personal material.

SKILL DRILL: NECESSITIES

A. FATAL: Name, age, address and occupation of victim. Time. Location. Driver(s) of vehicle(s) involved. Victim identified as driver, passenger or pedestrian. Violations. Background of victim. Mortuary handling body. (See textbook checklist, chapter 15.)

B. LIEUTENANT: Name, age, address, where stationed, previous rank. Date entered service. Length of service. Medals, awards, war service. Local educational background.

C. PROJECT: Location, purpose, cost, financing. Owners. Demolition involved. Over-all plan if any. Name of builders if available. Completion date.

D. BLAZE: Location, Extent of damages, injuries, deaths. Duration of fire before under control. Cause. (See textbook checklist, chapter 15.)

E. NEW: Name, address, age. Previous position and residence. Predecessor. Background of appointee.

F. GAME: Score. Decisive play. Outstanding players. (See textbook checklist, chapter 15.)

G. VERDICT: Name, offense tried for, verdict. Background of trial. Length of time jury was out. Length of trial. Date for sentencing. Minimum-maximum possible sentences. (See textbook checklist, chapter 15.)

H. DEATH: Name, age, address, occupation. Cause of death. Length of illness. Survivors. (See textbook checklist, chapter 15.)

I. CLINIC: Location. Reason for closing. Number of persons served. Facility that will serve the patients. Comments of people in neighborhood, staff members. History of clinic.

J. ZONE: Person or group making request. Proposed structure to be built. Date of hearing. Known opposition. Comments from those in neighborhood. Present status of neighborhood.

K. QUEEN: Name, age, home town, class status, major. Vote totals. Other candidates. Type of campaign conducted by winner. Major supporters (fraternities, independent groups, etc.). Comments by queen. Name of last year's queen. Date and location of ceremony.

L. CRIME: Totals. Largest number of crimes (robberies, burglaries, etc.). Comparison with past years. Largest categories of increase, decrease. Activities that were causes of the increase, decrease. Comments by police authorities and others involved.

M. SPLIT: Names, addresses, ages, occupations of plaintiff and defendant. Cause of action. Dependents. Settlement sought.

N. DAMAGE: Names, addresses, ages, occupations of plaintiff and defendant. Date, time, place of accident. Reason for suit. Amount of damages claimed. (See textbook checklist, chapter 15.)

O. METERS: Sponsor. Purpose of or reason for proposal. Public demand or pressure for the action if any. Comments by other city council members. Income loss to city if meters are removed. Sponsor's comments on this loss. Date meters were introduced. Cost.

NOTE: The suggested material by no means exhausts all possibilities. You and your students may have better lists. Encourage students to play this game, the reporter's game, of selecting a subject and trying to figure out what must go into the story.

What, they should ask themselves, are the absolutely necessary items that such a story must include? When they answer that question, they have a checklist that starts the reporting process.

In other words, as soon as an assignment is made, the reporter begins to think about the questions to ask so that the necessary information for the story may be gathered. The same process occurs at the writing.

This is one of the crucial concepts to press your students to understand. There are two necessary questions that determine much of the journalist's work:

1. What does this event demand that I put into my story?
2. What tone does this event have that must be reflected in the voice of the story?

As someone remarked, you can't write if you can't think. If the student can think through the dozens of twists and turns that occur at events with several speakers, the job is half over. The trick is to cut through the several ideas and the verbiage to find the main theme, the most important element. Here, the early chapters might be reviewed.

WORKBOOK

A good starter exercise is A. COUNCIL. Although this is a meeting story, it can represent this whole class of stories because it has a number of elements for the student to choose from. When this exercise was used with a group of beginning journalism students at Humboldt State University, most students led their stories with item 2, the dismissal of Banks. "Irregularities" sounded like theft to them. It could be simply bad arithmetic. But if it had been anything serious, the audit would have undoubtedly been in the news before this.

News Conferences - B. REJECT is moderately difficult. The subject, censorship, continues to pop up in the news. You might find some recent examples of groups trying to censor books.

Speeches - C. ASTROLOGY is fun. A lot of students are devoted followers of the zodiac and cannot resist trying to rebut the speaker in their news stories. I have read D. DRIVING aloud to students in the news writing laboratory toward the end of the semester. They seem to do well on this one. E. CECIL is a favorite of mine. I heard this on the radio in Canada several years ago and wrote Hunt for a copy. He is truly a funny man. You may have a lot of car-conscious young people in your class, and they might enjoy this.

NOTE: The all-time favorite news conference of veteran journalists is the Nixon concession in the 1962 California gubernatorial race. It was hardly a conference. Nixon let none of the reporters in the hotel lobby get in a word. If the students are up for it, try F. NIXON.

EXERCISES

A. Council

By this time, the student should be able to spot the most important elements of an event. Here, the fourth item, construction of sewers, seems the most important. Obviously, there are insufficient details for a full story here. The purpose is limited: to make certain the students know how to organize and structure a multiple-element story:

> The city council last night approved a referendum at the May election on a $1-million bond issue to finance the downtown sewer construction project.
> The proposal is the first step in the city's 10-year City Core Regeneration Plan. Traffic rerouting is next, and construction of a mall downtown is the third and final step.
> The present sewer system, in use since 1884, is inadequate for the city and sewage has been leaking into the ground water supply.
> The Council also took these actions:

> Viaduct....
> Dismissed Banks....
> Added Sanitation....

B. Reject

The story should begin with the rejection by five
school board members of the association's request,
thus sinking it. The legal issue is another significant item and belongs high in the copy. There are
many excellent quotes, and they should be used copi-
ously. Also, give the association's point of view
full attention. Here is a type of delayed lead students seem to like:

> Huck Finn will remain on the shelves of
> local school libraries and in classrooms.
> Five of the seven members of the city
> school board today indicated they will vote
> against a request to remove "The Adventures
> of Huckleberry Finn" and five other books....

C. Astrology

> A professor of physics at Mallory Col-
> lege said today that astrology is "quasi-
> scientific occultism."
> In his talk to the annual meeting of
> the College Science Club, Prof. Albert Sher-
> man said generally no harm is done by the
> belief.
> "But some people do take,..." he said.

Then continue with his distinction between sci-
ence and pseudoscience.
The story lends itself to a delayed lead also.
Here is one that seems fairly successful:

> "This is a good day for concluding the
> arrangement you have been thinking about,
> but avoid making too many commitments in your
> personal life at this time."

If you are a Gemini, this was your
horoscope in this morning's newspaper.
It's all perfectly harmless, says Prof.
Albert Sherman. But astrological advice
is no more realistic than the plots in
the newspaper's comic strips.

In fact, he said in a speech to the
College Science Club today, astrology is
"quasi-scientific occultism." Despite
this, "people take astrology seriously,"
he said. "They make business...."

Then go into his differentiation between science
and pseudoscience.

D. Driving

This speech can be focused around the speaker's advice: Make it tougher to give driver's licenses and
easier to take them away. That should be followed by
his specific recommendations on drunk driving penal-
ties.

E. Cecil

This talk was actually given on a program of the
Canadian Broadcasting Corp. in July 1979 and is being
used with the permission of the CBC and the author.
It struck me as a good example of that rarest of com-
modities, light humor. The best approach a student
can take is to quote extensively. Just introduce
Hunt with a delayed lead of some sort and let him
speak for himself.

F. Nixon

This is the famous good-bye speech of Richard Nixon,
his first one, when he lost to Pat Brown in California
in 1962. I have used the tape for many years as an
exercise in writing to deadline. Several instructors
find the transcript more useful with beginners.

It is not easy to capture the mood, much less to blend all the newsworthy elements, which are:

Nixon's concession.

The implied statement of retirement from politics.

The attack on the press.

The election background.

Here is the AP story:

Beverly Hills - AP - Richard M. Nixon admitted defeat in his bid for California's governorship today, congratulated the victor, then in an acidly bitter statement declared: "This is my last press conference."

The former Republican vice president did not elaborate on the remark, but in view of the crushing blow dealt to his political career by his loss to Governor Edmund G. Brown, it seemed apparent he intended it to mean he is bowing out of public life.

Nixon was trailing Democrat Brown by nearly 250,000 votes when he went before news conference microphones in mid morning and aired his views on political smears and on press and broadcast coverage of his long campaign.

After making his "last press conference" remark, Nixon told a big crowd of newsmen:

"You won't have Nixon to kick around much longer."

He looked drawn, and appeared grim during most of his talk. Once or twice he smiled a quick, tight smile, but his eyes at some points snapped with apparent anger. After concluding, he waved curtly and stalked away.

At one point in his nearly half-hour impromptu talk he remarked: "Thank God for radio and television. They will make papers more honest."

He devoted many of his words to news coverage of the campaign, but actually made few detailed allegations.

At one point he observed that in his last campaign speech "I made a flub by saying I was running for governor of the United States."

He said Brown made a verbal fluff that same day, urging election of Senator Thomas Kuchel when he obviously meant Republican Kuchel's Democratic opponent.

"The (Los Angeles) Times did not report it." Nixon said, "But it did report my flub." He said television reported both mistakes.

Frank McCulloch, day managing editor of the Los Angeles Times, said he wants to see a transcript of Nixon's remarks before making a statement.

Nixon said:

"My philosophy regarding the press has never gotten through...I think a reporter has the right, if he thinks one candidate ought to win, that he should say so.

"I might say I wish you had given my opponent the same going over as you gave me.

"You've had an opportunity to attack me. I've given as good as I've taken. You had a lot of fun.

"And I've had fun matching wits with you..."

Nixon had praise for what he called the fairness of Carl Greenberg, political writer for the Los Angeles Times, who he said reported the campaign fairly "despite whatever feelings he might have had, because he had an obligation to report everything."

The Times supported Nixon editorially.

At another point, Nixon said:

"Among the great newspapers people say I should be concerned about are the Louisville Courier, the New York Post, the Milwaukee Journal and the Sacramento and Fresno Bees.

"I couldn't disagree more. If newspapers are against a candidate, they should say it. But I think at least they should report what a candidate has to say."

Brown, who watched Nixon on television, said afterward:

"Nixon is going to regret all his life that he made that speech. The press will never let him forget it."

Mrs. Brown, at his side during a picture-posing

session at their home re-marked: "I'll be inter-ested to see the metropol-itan papers this afternoon to see what they carried about the speech."

Nixon told the news con-ference: "I congratulate Governor Brown for his victory. He has the greatest honor and the greatest responsibility of any governor in the United States...I wish him well."

Brown claimed victory at 1 a.m., but Nixon - still hoping for a turn in the tide - went to bed without making a statement.

Then about 10:20 a.m., after his press secre-tary, Herbert G. Klein, made the initial an-nouncement, Nixon strode to a battery of micro-phones and said:

"I believe Governor Brown has a heart even though he believes I do not....

"I believe he's a good American even though he believes I'm not....

"I want it to be known that I never during the course of the campaign raised a personal con-sideration against my opponent - I never accused him of a lack of heart, a lack of patriotism.

"You gentlemen (meaning the press) didn't report that I defended his patri-otism, that I said he was a man of good motives....

"For once, gentlemen, I would appreciate that you write it that way (that Nixon never attacked Brown personally)..."

Nixon started out by saying:

"Now that Mr. Klein has made his statement, and now that all the members of the press are so de-lighted that I have lost, I want to make one myself.

"I appreciated press coverage in this campaign. I think each of you wrote it the way you saw it. I think press men should write it that way.

"I don't think pub-lishers should order re-porters to write it one way or another."

"But, he added, he doesn't think the Federal Communications Commission should silence this "one voice raised in the wil-derness: in his behalf.

He was apparently re-ferring to an FCC order requiring a Los Angeles television station to give Democrats equal time because of allegedly par-tisan Nixon comments by two commentators.

85

A close reader of the transcript may find some of AP's quotes slightly off. This is a good opportunity to discuss the problems of deadline writing.

The New York Times reporter had more time. His newspaper needed his copy by mid afternoon for the first edition. But 3 p.m. in New York is noon in California time, so The Times reporter had to hustle also. He then had another couple of hours to smooth out his story for later editions. Here is how the Times story, by Gladwin Hill, began:

Beverly Hills, Calif., Nov. 7 - Richard M. Nixon conceded Defeat today. He later devoted what many observers regard as the possible valedictory of his national political career to a bitter denunciation of the press.

He also made some acid remarks about his victorious gubernatorial opponent, Gov. Edmund G. Brown, in a statement to about 100 newsmen at the Beverly Hilton Hotel here. The statement was his first public utterance since the election yesterday, which dashed the former Vice President's hopes of a political comeback.

A failure to win his native state had been widely assessed before the election as impair-ing, probably irreparably, the 49-year-old Republican's viability in national politics.

His defeat came by a vote margin six times as large as the margin by which he carried California in 1960, when he lost the Presidential election to John F. Kennedy. The virtually unanimous opinion of political observers was that the defeat had obliterated the lingering possibility, despite his disclaimers, that he might figure in the Presidential race of 1964.

In his denunciation of the press, Mr. Nixon said to the newsmen today, "You won't have Nixon to kick around any more, because, gentlemen, this is my last press conference."

After four more paragraphs of background, Hill gives a chronology of the returns:

Since yesterday afternoon, Mr. Nixon had been in a seventh-floor suite of the hotel, scrutinizing election returns.

At 2:30 a.m. local time (5:30 a.m. Eastern Standard Time), his press secretary,....

Then Hill takes Nixon downstairs:

Mr. Nixon looked very tired. His voice quavered at several points in

what turned out to be a 15-minute monologue....

Next, Hill gives the reader many quotes.

You might obtain a copy of the full story from the Times microfilm for the class.

In her column, Mary McGrory wrote this lead: For Richard Nixon, it was exit snarling.

There are too many subjects in this chapter to cram
into a week or two of writing work. But you may want
to select an exercise now and then during the semester.

WORKBOOK

EXERCISES I: ACCIDENTS

A.   Pedestrian

    James Reynolds, 48, of 35 W. Borden Ave.,
was critically injured yesterday when he was
struck by an automobile at Johnson and Elm
Streets.
    Reynolds, a sign painter, was taken to
Fairlawn Hospital where he was placed in intensive care. His injuries include a frac-
ture of the skull.
    The police said the driver of the vehicle
that struck Reynolds, Robert F. Magione, 872
Ogden St., told them Reynolds stepped into the
path of the vehicle. No charges were filed.

B.   Three Dead

    Mr. and Mrs. Stanley Shaeffer of 45
Marvell Ave. and their 17-year-old granddaughter, Anne, who was visiting her grandparents
before going to college, were killed last
night in a collision on Route 16 and State
Highway 40, 18 miles north of the city.
    The Shaeffer car was traveling on Route
16 and had just entered Highway 40 when it
collided with a car driven by Louis Kruger
of Hutchinson, Kan. Kruger suffered frac-
tures of a leg and internal injuries and was
taken to Fullerton Hospital.

Investigating Officers Albert Doris
and Ben Sandler said Shaeffer, 68, apparently had failed to stop at the stop
sign on Route 16. There is a possibility
he suffered a stroke, the officers said.
Miss Shaeffer was from Chicago and
was enroute to Boston University where she
was enrolled as a freshman.

Some editors demand in the lead the names and addresses of local persons injured or killed in motor
vehicle accidents. As we see in this story, this
tends to make the lead long. If the editor will accept a more general lead, the following would be more
succinct:

A local couple and their 17-year-old
granddaughter, who was visiting them before going to college, were killed last
night in a collision at Route 16 and State
Highway 40.
The police identified the victims
as:....

This lead is still a bit long, but shortening it
would eliminate the poignant aspect - the 17-year-old
who had stopped to see her grandparents on her way to
college. Certainly, we would not want a lead that
says: Three persons were killed last night....That
would be short enough, but it would eliminate the
human interest and pathos. This might be a good opportunity to remind the class of Othman's advice about
nouns that are the names of specific things. "Grandparents" and "granddaughter" summon up specific images
with which every reader is familiar.

C. Truck

Here, the lead element is the young man being crushed by his own truck.

> Irwin Soto, 22, of Clovia was killed today when his truck slipped off a jack and crushed him as he was repairing a tire.
>
> Police said Soto, who runs a dairy farm, apparently was killed instantly. The accident occurred four miles west of the city on an access road where he had stopped.
>
> Soto had been a star athlete in high school....
>
> He is survived by....
>
> The body is at the Clovia Funeral Home. Services are pending.

EXERCISE II: FIRES

A. Suspicious

Watch out for the possible libelous reference to Chip Ramsgate, the dishwasher the cafe owner suspects set the fire. There are no charges filed against Ramsgate. He cannot be mentioned in the story, but the lead should focus on the suspected arson:

> Officials suspect arson in a fire that forced 20 diners to leave the Crosson Cafe, 127 Dakota St., last night.
>
> The fire broke out shortly after 8 p.m. in the basement, sending dense black clouds of smoke into the restaurant. There were no injuries.
>
> "We were having steaks when suddenly the smoke started coming up through the floor and around the walls," said Scott Ryan, 1580 East Millerton Ave., who was dining with a friend, Kelly Serpa of 46 Barton St. Serpa

said some woman screamed but all she wor-
ried about was that her rare steak "was
going to be well done."

Ralph Crosson, owner of the restaurant, estimated damage at $15,000. He
said he is covered by insurance. He said
he recently fired an employee who vowed
to "get even." Police would not say
whether the former worker is a suspect.

EXERCISES III: POLICE AND CRIME

A. Drugs

The story printed in the workbook is taken from a New
England newspaper. The names have been changed. Your
students should spot the impersonation and footrace
angles quickly for the lead. Maybe something like
this will turn up:

A Biddeford youth lost a footrace to
sheriff's officers yesterday when he sought
to pick up drugs he had allegedly ordered
from a local pharmacy by posing as a physician.

If you prefer a delayed lead on this story, which
does lend itself to one, the lead and next paragraphs
could be:

A Biddeford youth fooled no one when
he allegedly sought to obtain narcotics from
the Stuben Drug Store yesterday.

The police said Mark Reib, 18, called
the store, identified himself as a Biddeford
physician, and said a messenger would pick
up the drugs he ordered.

Instead, police were waiting, and when
he left the drug store, they gave chase down
Main Street....

B.   Arrested

Carl Morton, who had been sought for six days in connection with the death of a 47-year-old pianist, was arrested today in a downtown hotel.

Police said Morton, who is 35 years old and has a prison record for robbery and possession of drugs, did not resist arrest.

Morton was sought in the slaying of Mildred Miller, who lived in the same hotel, The Plaza at 912 Washington Ave., where Morton had a room.

Det. Sgt. Richard Raskover said Morton will be questioned about the deaths of four elderly women who had lived in the hotel and died within the last six months under unusual circumstances.

Information from Morton's girl friend aided the police. Mrs. Miller's radio was found in Morton's room. Police said Morton's girl friend told them he had left the night of the slaying after depositing the radio in their room. He told her he had just sold a television set and was going out to purchase some food. He warned her not to tell anyone about the radio and television set. A radio and television set were missing from Mrs. Miller's room.

The police said that the victim had been strangled, raped, and her bed set afire....

NOTE: You may want to discuss the question of the use of Morton's arrest record. Would that prejudice his prospect for a fair trial? Another problem comes up in connection with the use of arrest records. In Morton's case, his arrests led to convictions. But many arrests do not. The cases are dismissed. Is it fair to refer in a news story to arrests not followed by convictions? Many states have laws that would strike from a person's records any arrest that did not result in conviction. The basis of the legislators' thinking is that an arrest is nothing more than an accusation of criminal misconduct and that many times innocent people are arrested by mistake or falsely accused of a crime they did not commit.

C. Drowning

This drowning has three unusual aspects, any one of which could be considered for a lead or major emphasis:

The good turn of the couple, which, in a sense, set the scene for the soldier's death.

The discovery of the body by Russian swimmers.

The statement to the police of Mrs. Goodenow that she saw someone swimming around 3 or 4 a.m. and presumed it was one of the Russians swimming.

Most students who have handled this exercise have emphasized the first angle, the good turn that leads to tragedy.

DIRECT LEAD: A soldier on the way from Korea to reassignment was found dead at the bottom of a motel swimming pool here early today after a couple at the motel had let him share their room for the night.

DELAYED LEAD: An act of friendship offered by a young couple from Denver, here to celebrate their first wedding anniversary, turned to tragedy.

The soldier they allowed to share their motel room was found dead this morning in the swimming pool of the Beach and Oceanaire Motel at 4217 E. Ocean Blvd.

A delayed lead is acceptable since the soldier's identification is not essential in Long Beach. In his home town, the story would require a direct lead.

Many students who wrote the story straight had leads of this sort:

> The body of a young soldier, the apparent victim of an accidental drowning, was found early this morning at the bottom of a swimming pool at the Beach and Oceanaire Motel at 4217 E. Ocean Blvd.
>
> The victim was identified by Long Beach police as Nathaniel Frazier, 22, who was en route from Korea to Ft. Bragg, N.C. He was found at 6:30 a.m. by Alexi Morrisev, one of a group of Russian swimmers staying at the motel.

There is nothing incorrect about the way this story begins. But it does miss the drama and the unique aspects of this particular drowning.

Be wary of those who push the drama too far. A few students can be counted on to write that the Colorado couple caused the soldier's death, and I have had one or two--investigative reporters in the making, perhaps--who concluded that the couple made the soldier drunk and did him in, as a result of some bizarre racial-sexual rite.

When the exercise was first used in the early 1970s, many students emphasized the fact that a <u>white</u> couple was doing a <u>black</u> soldier a good turn and that this was unusual. With the years, the racial aspect dropped away. It is legitimate, however, to raise the question of whether race is relevant anywhere in this story. You may want to discuss the guidelines for use of race in a news story. The textbook discusses this.

NOTE: Some of the more enterprising students might discover mistakes in the police report. For example: Under Residence Address, the police have made it: USERPAC. This is a typo. It is USARPAC, which stands for United States Army of the Pacific. Also, some of the designations are no longer used. Remind the students that this is not the current army. Frazier has no rank; call him a soldier.

D. Cookies

Anything, almost, goes on a story of this sort. Here is one version:

> Was it worth it?
> Somewhere in town today a burglar must be asking himself that question.
> Sometime last night, the basement of the United Methodist Church at 850 Johnson St. was broken into and a large carton removed.
> The basement is used by the Central Berkshire Regional School District as a day-care center, and the carton contained cookies for the children's milk break.
> But the children wouldn't eat them. Too stale, they said. The center was planning to return the cookies.

E. Crime Reports

There are two ways to handle this story: for general readership interested in the precinct figures and for a university readership interested in the police post figures.

For a general readership:

> Crime rose slightly in the northwestern section of the city last year, but it did not approach the totals of three years ago.

Police reported 1,844 crimes in the
18th Precinct, compared with 1,753 two
years ago and 3,299 the previous year.
Two-thirds of last year's crimes were
burglaries and thefts from motor vehicles.

Most of the increase of 91 crimes
last year over the preceding year were
reported in Police Post No. 3, where the
university is located. Crime reported
last year in the post rose to 220 from
148 two years ago.

Capt. Stanley Solomon of the 18th
Precinct, which includes Post No. 3, said
the precinct-wide increases were due main-
ly to property thefts, which the figures
reveal to be surging.

This is a city-wide trend, Capt.
Colomon said....(Quote him.)

For a university readership:

Crimes reported in the university
area last year rose 50 percent over the
previous year, police reported today.

A combination lead could be:

Crime rose slightly last year in
the northwestern part of the city, almost
all of the increase occurring in the
university area.

F. Bite

This story is used at the School of Journalism of the
University of Colorado. Here is the sample story:

A police dog bit the hand that feeds
him last night and let an intruder escape.

Sheridan police officer William Trevor reported he heard an intruder enter his apartment at 1250 Humboldt St., Denver, at about 12:45 a.m. and took his police revolver to investigate. When Trevor pointed the gun at the intruder, his police dog, Rusty, apparently got excited and bit Trevor instead of the intruder.

Trevor is in good condition in Denver General Hospital with deep bites on his right wrist. Rusty was held for observation. The intruder, described as a white male, bare-foot, wearing blue jeans and a Mickey Mouse T-shirt, escaped and is being sought by police.

EXERCISES IV: OBITUARIES

A. Ibbotson

Mrs. Agnes Viola Ibbotson, 85, of 7101 Twana Dr., Urbandale, a former resident of Burlington, died at her home at 8:02 p.m. Tuesday, April 13.

The daughter of Harry and Elizabeth Hines McDonald, she was born Sept. 5, 1890, at Morning Sun. She married Eugene Burton Ibbotson in October 1912; he died in November 1948.

She was a member of Grace United Methodist Church of Burlington.

Surviving: Two sons, Donald, Mason City, and Gene, Des Moines; four daughters, Arlene Walker, Urbandale, Vera Gibbs, West Burlington, and Gladys Goss and Verlee Johnson, both of Burlington; brother John McDonald, Morning Sun; 16 grandchildren; and 21 great-grandchildren.

Funeral: 2:30 Friday, Lunning Chapel, the Rev. Leroy Moore; Kossuth cemetery.

B.   Perkins

In this obituary, the accomplishments of the deceased
should be played up, his presidency of the bar association and his chairmanship of the local chapter of
the National Foundation for Infantile Paralysis. Apparently his widow is his only survivor. You might
discuss the wording of the request not to send flow-
ers.

     William F. Perkins of 1105 Madison Ave.,
a former president of the state bar association and for many years active with the local
chapter of the National Foundation for Infantile Paralysis, died yesterday at the age of
73 following a heart attack.
     Perkins was associated with the law firm
of O'Connor & Perkins. He was a graduate of
Harvard Law School where he was a member of
the Law Review. He was born in Altoona, Pa.
     He is survived by his widow, Josephine
Parker Perkins, who requested that remem-
brances be donated to the Community Hospital
Medical Center.
     The body is at the Geo. T. Smith mortu-
ary. Visiting hours are 7 to 9 p.m. Tuesday.
The services will be held at the funeral
home, 14 Laura Place, 10 a.m. Wednesday.

C.   Tsouprake

     Dr. Demetrios Athanasias Tsouprake,
internationally known patent and copyright
attorney, died of cancer last night in Community General Hospital. He was 75 years
old and lived at 560 Maple St.
     In 1958, Dr. Tsouprake was a United
States delegate to the conference in Lisbon
to revise the international treaty on pa-
tents. In 1968 he received the Robert Kent

Award of the Patent, Trademark and Research
Institute of Oxford University for meritor-
ious work. His books included "Protection
of Industrial Property" and "Protection of
Literary and Artistic Property."

He was born in Athens, Greece, received
an LL.D. degree from Athens University, an
A.M. degree from the School of Political
Science in Paris, and an LL.B. degree from
Stanford.

Survivors include his wife, the former
Juliana Lappas; two daughters, Natalie Ar-
ruzel of Florence, Italy, and Christine A.
Costa of New York; and four grandchildren.

Funeral services will be held Wednesday at 11 a.m. in the Greek Orthodox Cathe-
dral of the Holy Trinity.

D. Longo

There are several angles in this story: the Italian
immigrant who made a great success of his life although he had no formal education, the creation of
the Longo System and the $580,000 estate, much of
which goes to the local public library. Some possibilities:

Frank Longo, 78, formerly of 465 Lief
Ave., a self-educated Italian immigrant who
devised an inventory system for a local concern that was used by businesses around the
country, died yesterday in San Jose, Costa
Rica, following a heart attack.

Or:

Frank Longo, who lived out the American story of the immigrant boy who made good,

died yesterday in San Jose, Costa Rica, at
the age of 78. He had been employed here
by the B.C. Krebs Manufacturing Co. as a
personnel manager.

Or:

    Frank Longo, retired personnel manager
for the B.C. Krebs Manufacturing Co., died
yesterday in Costa Rica at the age of 78.
He left most of his $580,000 estate to the
city public library system, which he described as his high school, college and
graduate school.

  Four of five students select the first lead, em-
phasizing the Longo System. I think it is the weak-
est lead, since the computer has obviously made ob-
solete traditional inventory systems. The enterprising student (one of 10) may notice that Longo initiated a non-discriminatory hiring system at the B.C.
Krebs company, when he was 57. If the student sub-
tracts 57 from Longo's age at death, 78, the student
will see that the system was adopted 21 years ago,
which was well before the anti-discrimination laws.
The result could be a lead like this:

    Frank Longo, formerly of 465 Lief Ave.,
a self-educated Italian immigrant who was a
pioneer in eliminating discrimination in
hiring in a local manufacturing concern, died
yesterday in San Jose, Costa Rica.

  Note that in the second paragraph of the release
"immigrating" is used. "Emigrating" is proper.

EXERCISES V: SPORTS

A. Runner

Make sure the student brings in Mallory's success at
the NCAA meet, but does not lead with it as the story
of the meet would have been published right after
the event. This is an interview and is supposed to
be about the runner Baron. There are several possible lead angles: his strenuous training, pack-
running as a tactic, the scholar-athlete aspect of
the team and school. Then go into Helmer's remarks.
Blend the results of the meet into the ongoing interview, which can be done with a phrase like this in
the second paragraph:

> Baron, who finished eleventh in the NCAA
> Division III meet in Boston and helped his
> team to a fourth-place finish, said....

B. Trade

If your city is not a cool area, then tell the students to imagine they are working in Montreal. Tell
your students the players' names are fictitious and
the facts accurate. A delayed lead would probably
be demanded by many sports editors, something like
this:

> Willie Suarez finally is going to warmer
> climes where he thinks his bat will be hotter.
> After a season and a half with the Red
> Sox, the unhappy outfielder was traded to the
> Atlanta Braves for a utility infielder and a
> reserve outfielder.
> Last year, although he didn't like the
> cool weather here, he batted .310 and drove
> in 101 runs. After 50 games this season, he
> was batting .274, respectable enough, but his
> RBI total of 20 was anemic.

A club official was not sorry to see
Suarez go, although he admitted the Puerto
Rican slugger is a fine hitter.
"He's got great potential, but he'll
kill his career with this kind of attitude,"
the official said.
In return for Suarez, a veteran of three
seasons in Philadelphia and one in windswept
Candlestick Park with the Giants, the Red Sox
received Dave Martin, an infielder who is
batting .246, and George White, an outfielder
batting .265. Asked why the potential of
Suarez brought so little in trade, an official
replied:
"Well, you might say...."

C.   Reds-Braves

Some instructors wanted a ball game of some kind so
that students could learn to make a box score and
write an account. This imaginary game involves two
teams with National League names.

Have the students talk it over first and see how,
as Red Smith would say, this game differs from all
other ball games. Here are some points:

Katz: His first win over the Braves this season. His
first complete game this season. He's the winner
though he was in trouble in every inning.

Reds: The win puts them to within a game of the
Braves for the league lead.

Clearly, this was a pitcher's duel, the kind of
game old-timers enjoy watching. Here are some leads:

Art Katz pitched the Reds a game closer to the division-leading Braves last night,
beating Carl Lemon in a pitcher's duel, 2-1.

Art Katz, who was in trouble in every inning last night, pitched his first complete game of the season for the Reds, beating the Braves 2-1.

Art Katz overcame Braves runners in every inning and a blister on his throwing hand to best Carl Lemon in a pitching duel last night 2-1. The win put the Reds within a game of the league-leading Braves.

Ron Rapoport, who covers sports for the Chicago Sun-Times, put color and drama in this version of the game.

Eleven hits didn't stop him. Runners on base in every inning didn't stop him. It was hardly to be expected, therefore, that Art Katz would be stopped short of his first complete game of the season by something as insignificant as a blister on his pitching hand.

The Reds' right-hander finally achieved his goal of being around at the end of a ballgame last night when his team beat the Braves, 2-1, to move within one game of the visiting league-leaders.

Johnny Gougeon's run-scoring single that dropped between two outfielders in center field in the seventh inning was the winning run, but it was Katz who was the key man in this victory.

In winning his eighth game of the season, Katz survived trouble in every inning as the Braves had runners on base in every inning. But the Braves could score only one run on a sacrifice fly by shortstop Maury Vorobil in the fifth.

In the eighth inning, Katz may have had his toughest job of the evening - convincing the Reds to let him stay in the game.

With two outs and the tying run on second base, everything stopped when Reds' catcher Chuck Marwell came to the mound. He took one look at the blister developing on a finger on Katz' pitching hand and called for the trainer. The ensuing conference ended with Katz insisting he could finish the game....

For the box score, here is the style some newspapers use. You may want to make additions and alterations as you see fit.

BOX SCORE

BRAVES	ab	r	h	bi	REDS	ab	r	h	bi
Bumiller cf	4	0	2	0	Eddings ss	4	0	0	0
Vorobil ss	4	0	1	1	Manoff lf	3	1	1	1
Weiner rf	4	0	1	0	Douge 3b	2	1	0	0
Wallis lf	3	0	2	0	Cruz 1b	3	0	1	0
Hand 3b	3	0	0	0	Marwell c	3	0	0	0
Sherman 1b	3	0	0	0	Gougeon cf	2	0	1	1
Day c	4	0	2	0	Kelso 2b	3	0	0	0
Weir 2b	4	1	2	0	Barrett rf	3	0	1	0
Lemon p	2	0	0	0	Katz p	3	0	0	0
Ahearn ph	1	0	1	0					
	32	1	11	1		26	2	4	2

```
Braves   000 010 000 - 1 11 0
Reds     000 100 10X - 2  4 1
```
E - Kelso; LOB - Braves 8, Reds 2;
2B - Wallis, Barrett; HR - Manoff (15);
SB - Wallis; S - Hand, Lemon; SF - Vorobil.

	IP	H	R	ER	BB	SO
Lemon (11-4)	8	4	2	2	1	2
Katz (8-4)	9	11	1	1	3	4

HBP - by Lemon (Gougeon).
T - 2:04. A - 16,069

D. Loser

Most sports editors of morning newspapers would want
a feature lead on a game played the previous afternoon
since most fans will know the score and winning and
losing pitchers by the next day. A lead that editors
might accept would run something like this:

> The nothing pitcher won again yester-
> day, leaving the Red Sox leading hitter, Ted
> Schmidt, full of pity for Randy Jones, who
> fanned him twice as Schmidt went zero for
> four.
> "If I were a pitcher I'd be embarrassed
> to go to the mound with the kind of stuff
> Jones has. A nothing pitcher. Nothing."
> Delivering himself of this opinion fol-
> lowing his fruitless day at the plate in the
> Sox 2-0 loss to the Phillies, Schmidt kicked
> his locker and lapsed into silence.
> Manager Danny Appel, who takes the long
> view of things, could understand Schmidt's
> frustration.
> "A lot of guys say...," he said.

Next summarize the game, then the standings.

SKILL DRILL: SPORTS VOCABULARY

Baseball

A. MVP: Most Valuable Player. Award made each year
    in National and American Leagues by the Baseball
    Writers Association. (And in other sports as well.)
B. PINCH RUNNER: A substitute sent in to run for a
    player who is on base, usually because the player
    is a slow runner and the potential run he repre-
    sents may be crucial to the game.
C. SACRIFICE FLY: A fly ball that advances a runner
    home. The batter is not credited with a time at
    bat.

D. SAVE: A designation for a game that a relief pitcher saves--by holding the lead--for the previous pitcher.
E. SCRATCH HIT: A hit that is the result of fast running, slow fielding, or the effect of the field on a ball. Usually, the scratch hit is a grounder that does not move past the infield.
F. TEXAS LEAGUER: A looping or arching fly ball that drops between the infielders and the out-fielders for a base hit.

Basketball

A. DUNK SHOT: Placing the ball through the hoop by leaping above the rim and thrusting the ball down-ward through the hoop.
B. GIVE AND GO: A play in which one player passes to another and goes directly to the basket where he expects a return pass.
C. NIT: National Invitational Tournament.
D. TOP OF THE KEY: The area in the circle of the free-throw line.
E. TRAILER: A player who trails the offensive team as it breaks toward the basket. As the defensive team covers the fast-running players, the ball may be passed back to the trailer for an unopposed attempt at the basket.
F. ZONE DEFENSE: The method of defense whereby a player is responsible for guarding an area rather than a man. Used in college basketball, but banned in the professional game.

Football

A. FLANKER: The player stationed wide left or right of the line of scrimmage as a pass receiver.
B. FLARE OUT: A player who runs to the far side, or any wide area, to receive a pass. The player is said to flare out.
C. BLITZ: A tactic of the defense whereby players rush the offensive quarterback, usually when he is planning to pass.

D. SACK: The tackling of the offensive quarterback,
    usually as he is waiting to pass to potential re-
    ceivers in a pass play.
E. TIGHT END: The offensive end who is placed close
    to the line of scrimmage. (Note: This skill
    drill was given to a class and one student de-
    fined this term as: "Marilyn Monroe in a bikini."
    The drill may not be fair to students who are un-
    familiar with sports.)

Golf

A. EAGLE: A score of two shots under par on a hole.
    Holing in two on a par-four hole would be an
    eagle. Taking three shots on a par-four hole
    would be a birdie.
B. PGA: Professional Golfer's Association.
C. PAR-FOUR HOLE: A hole designated as needing four
    strokes to sink the ball in the cup.
D. SLICE: The flight of the ball that curves to the
    right of a right-handed player, to the left of a
    left-handed player. (The opposite effect is
    called a hook, a ball that deviates from a straight
    course in a direction opposite from the player's
    dominant hand.)

Hockey

A. FACE OFF: The dropping of the puck between two
    opposing players to initiate play.
B. HIGH STICKING: Carrying stick above the shoulders
    and using it to strike opposing players. Results
    in penalty if detected.
C. ICING: Shooting puck from behind red line into
    opponent's zone or shooting it length of ice.
    Play is stopped and restarted in zone from which
    puck was hit. All right if team that hits puck
    is short handed by penalty.
D. RED LINE: Line marked on ice between center area
    and blue line.

E. SUDDEN DEATH: A game that ends in a tie goes into a sudden death overtime in which the first
team to score wins. Used in playoff games. (Used
in other sports, especially football.)

Tennis

A. ACE: A serve that is not returned by the opposing
player.
B. DOUBLE FAULT: Two serves that are illegal, the
serving player losing the point.
C. MIXED DOUBLES: Four players; male and female on
each side.
D. PASSING SHOT: A return with such velocity that it
goes by the opposing player.

Thoroughbred Horse Racing

A. CLAIMER: A horse entered in a claiming race for
a price at which it will be sold to the person
claiming the horse. The claim is made before the
race, and the horse is sold after the race, whatever the result or the condition of the horse.
B. FRACTIONS: The times a horse has run sections of
the race, usually the first quarter of a mile,
the half mile, six furlongs (six-eighths of a
mile), mile, etc.
C. MAIDEN RACE: A race for horses that have never
won a race.
D. STRETCH RUNNER: A horse that prefers to stay behind for most of the race (to stay off the pace)
and then accelerates in the last straightaway,
which is called the stretch.
E. TURF RACE: A race conducted over grass. Most
races in the United States are run over a dirt
track.

EXERCISE VI: PRECEDES

A. Planning

  The city planning board meeting
scheduled for tomorrow night has been put
off until next Tuesday because of the
death of Alice Nicholson, wife of the
board chairman, Philip Nicholson.

B. Parade

  The downtown area will be turned over
to the youngsters Sunday, May 7.
  The annual Kiddies Day Parade will
begin at 1 p.m. at Elm and Johnson Avenues
and will wind through the city's business
district.
  Mayor Sam Parnass will lead the parade, carrying his one-year-old daughter,
Candy. All other youngsters are expected
to do their own parading. Last year,
about 200 three to eight year olds took
part.
  The destination is the First Congrega-
tional Church where judges will make awards
for....

C. Recital

This exercise is deceptive. Obviously, the pianist
cannot play all of Chopin's mazurkas and etudes in
one recital. Make it "several of" or "some of...."
Also, Liszt is misspelled as List.

D. Appreciation

This exercise has been adapted from a story that appeared in the <u>Louisville Courier-Journal</u>. Some of
the names have been changed.

Tom Slinkard has made 51 parachute jumps from an airplane without an injury.

But now he's nursing a broken leg he got when he tripped off his back steps at his home, 2815 Yorkshire Blvd.

So Slinkard, president of the Southwest Parachute Association, won't be going along tomorrow when three other association members are scheduled to drop some 4,500 feet at Patterson Field Appreciation Day Sunday.

The free-falling jumps are to be a part of an afternoon of events saluting one of the nation's busiest private airports.

The program, sponsored by the local Junior Chamber of Commerce aviation committee, will open at 1 p.m. with an hour of plane rides for the public. Passengers will pay for the rides at the rate of a penny a pound for their weight.

At 1:50 p.m., the state commissioner of aeronautics, William Sullivan, is scheduled to land a plane with Lieutenant Governor Harry Lee Waterfield aboard to open an hour of demonstrations. Crop dusting and spraying and the parachute jumps will be among the demonstrations.

Airplane rides will be given again from 3 to 6 p.m. At 4 p.m., the Sports Car Club will give an exhibition of skill driving at the southeast corner of the field.

Some 30 aircraft will be on display throughout the day in front of the Administration Building. Patterson Field was opened in 1939. Since the field has been in operation, there have been more than a million landings and takeoffs without a fatality.

This is a prototype story. That is, it is typical of the type in which a person proficient in an area is felled by an accident or an affliction one would expect the expert to be able to avoid--the lifeguard drowning in a bathtub; the fireman whose home catches fire; here, the parachutist who can't manage his back steps. Most editors would want the story written this way.

There is a question of fairness involved, however, and I would suggest discussing this with the class. A lifeguard can have a stroke while bathing and die in his tub. A parachutist's daughter can leave a roller skate on the steps and her dad can do a double-somersault no matter how agile he may be. An alternative lead could be the penny-a-pound flights. It's not as humorous, but Slinkard would be spared embarrassment.

Avoid leads playing up the commissioner's or lieutenant governor's visit. Students should be told that these are routine activities of officials. Watch out for publicity puffs of hyperbole and over-enthusiasm. Of course, the piece is publicity of a sort. But this is the kind of public-service story newspapers publish all the time. Many families, and some airplane and sports car enthusiasts, will want to go out to the field on Sunday.

E.   Poets

Lead with Merrill, a Pulitzer Prize poet. He also won the National Book Award for poetry. You could give this as a home assignment and ask students to use reference materials.

F.   Lobby

A 10-member delegation from the local chapter of the League of Women Voters will be buttonholing state legislators at the statehouse Monday in opposition to a minimum wage bill.
       The bill would exempt....
       "The bill clearly is aimed...."

111

G. Trip

The lead angle here is the unusual situation of an
airlines clerk never leaving the country until his
retirement. A delayed lead would work well:

>   Dale L. Himmelstein was a clerk for the
> United Airlines for 30 years until his re-
> tirement but had never left his home state.
>   But since he left the airline three
> years ago he has more than made up for his
> lack of travel abroad. On July 15, he and
> Mrs. Himmelstein, 42 Ft. Washington Ave.,
> leave for Russia. A month later, they will
> be traveling to China.
>   This will be the 21st and 22nd....

EXERCISES VII: PERSONALS

A. Merit

An interesting question arises here. Do you stress in
the lead that a handicapped youngster has won a Merit
Scholarship? Or should that be played down? It might
be interesting to have the class discuss this first.
One possible way of handling the story:

>   Patricia Elman, 18, of 1716 Palisades
> Ave. has won a National Merit Scholarship
> that she plans to use to study pre-medicine
> at the University of Texas in Austin.
>   Elman is the city's only Merit Scholar.
> Her scholarship is worth $3,000.
>   Elman, who was confined to bed in her
> freshman and sophomore years and has been
> in a wheelchair since her junior year, is
> one of 3,500 Merit Scholars in the country....

B.   District Attorney

District Attorney Paul Robinson will
tell fellow prosecutors at a national conference about the career-criminal tracking
system he initiated here.
     Robinson will speak July 23 in Chicago
to the National Conference of Prosecutors.
The system is designed to identify the fre-
quent offender on arrest so that plea bar-
gaining--allowing the defendant to plead
guilty to a lesser charge--is avoided.

EXERCISE VIII: LOCALIZING

A. Appointees

This exercise should demonstrate how the audience de-
termines the nature of the story.

1. Boston readers will want to know about the ap-
    pointment of Norton. The story should not men-
    tion Adams.

         Gerald P. Norton, 35, a native of West
    Roxbury, Mass., was appointed today to the
    newly created position of deputy general
    counsel to the Federal Trade Commission.
         Norton received an A.B. degree....

     (Notice that there is no attribution in the lead.
It is not necessary.)

2. Lexington, Ky., readers would be told about the
    appointment of Adams, and this story should follow
    the same style as the Norton story.
3. The AP story would name both, give the home cities
    of each and presume that local newspapers would
    rewrite the story, adding information on their own
    about their local men. The AP story would run no
    more than a couple of paragraphs.

EXERCISE IX: ROUNDUP

A.   Pot

You may find this a worthwhile exercise in organizing
material and finding the lead, which is buried.   I
would use as the lead the danger of "irreversible
brain damage" to the habitual user.
        Research in this area is progressing rapidly and
you may want your students to bring the research up
to date.   One of the major active components of marijuana, the acid THC, has a chemical makeup similar
to estrogen, and some research has been done that indicates that estrogen administered to some women has
been carcinogenic.   That is, estrogen can cause cancer.
Experiments have been carried out showing that large
doses of marijuana have estrogen-like effects on mice.
        Experiments by Army researchers have shown that
male mice given large doses of marijuana develop
smaller-than-normal testicles and became less potent
than normal.

EXERCISES X: WEATHER

A.   Wind

        Winds whipping up to 50 miles an hour
damaged residences and businesses on State
Road 166 near Clovia last night.
        Damages totalled $15,000, mostly to
outbuildings in the suburban area.   The
Crossroads Grocery at Three Corners suffered $5,000 in damages when the winds,
which struck around 11 p.m., blew out the
glass in the store and shook merchandise
from the shelves.   There were no injuries.

B.   Cold

        The temperature reached a 15-year low
for this day at 5 o'clock this morning.
The temperature dipped to 25 degrees.

This was the third straight day of unseasonably cold weather. But the weather bureau says that the cold snap should end by tonight.

The all-time low for the day was 15 degrees in 1880. The all-time high was 69 degrees in 1945.

C. Rain

This may not rate as much of a disaster, but students should have some experience writing about natural calamities. A big rain in the southwest can be a serious matter, especially if it should strike in a canyon area. Here is how the UPI began its story of the Houston rain:

Houston - UPI - A torrential summer storm poured more than seven and a half inches of rain on the city in seven hours today, spilling creeks and bayous out of their banks, flooding streets, and stranding motorists during the rush hour.

For the first time in the 11-year history of the Astrodome, the Astros had to call off a baseball game, not because the field under the dome was wet, but because fans could not reach the stadium.

One of the hardest hit areas was the....

16   LIBEL, ETHICS AND TASTE

In libel, ethics and taste there is more uncertainty than certainty. A word is spelled correctly or it is not. A verb agrees with the subject or it does not. The lead is on target or it is buried. But now we are adrift in a sea of uncertainties.

Judges are constantly changing their minds about such matters as the definition of a public figure, what constitutes the invasion of privacy and the nature of libelous language. For an instructor, the task is made more difficult by the desire to warn of the dangers of libel but to avoid frightening the student so that he or she is made passive. We need an assertive journalism.

Perhaps you can begin the libel discussion by asking students to clip material they consider libelous. You may find them confused, even timid about matters. Generally, what they see in print is perfectly safe. You can introduce the concept of privilege this way.

As for ethics, most students are torn between the desire to want absolutes and the realization that there are few in the affairs of men and women. I do not believe we have to go so far as to admit to situational ethics, that there are no rules--just do what is proper in each situation. I do stress some absolutes. You may want to add others in a class discussion.

I would hope students can be guided by some internal compass rather than by the weather vane, shifting with each slight change of the wind.

Each one to his own taste, says the French expression. That won't do. Again, we need guidelines. And again, one way to start the students is to have them bring to class material that they consider profane, obscene or tasteless. You might lead them to some conclusions in your class discussion.

As you may conclude from the text, I consider it most important that the student establish for himself or herself a personal code. I have found that no imposed code is as influential as the reporter's own.

Here are some guidelines for libel you might want to pass on to your students:

Guidelines to Avoid Libel

Most libel suits, or at least the successful ones, could be avoided by observing the following rules:

1. The story should not be colored by the enthusiasms or opinions of the reporter.
2. The statements of police or other informants made outside of court must be taken with caution; and where the story is of a defamatory kind, must be verified so far as practicable.
3. The truth is a defense, but good intention in reporting an untruth is not.
4. A retraction is not a defense. It serves only to lessen damages and to deprive the plaintiff of the recovery of punitive damages. "Punitive damages" is an amount assessed by way of punishment, and goes beyond the mere actual loss suffered by the plaintiff.
5. Safe reporting sticks to the facts, and not to some bystander's opinion of what might be the truth if the facts were known.

Our federal and state constitutions preserve the right freely to publish and to make comments, but every reporter, copy reader, rewrite man and editor should always keep in mind that published statements must be truthful and also that published comments must be fair, unbiased, uncolored and fully supported by the facts.

WORKBOOK

DISCUSSION

A. Libel and Privacy

1. The charges are not privileged since they were
    not made in Congress. Obviously, if the reporter
    has proof that the Republican candidate was in-
    deed a "failed businessman" - say, a record of
    his having filed a petition of bankruptcy - then
    the charges of being a "failed businessman" could
    be used since truth is a defense.
2. Whatever is said at a trial is privileged. Here,
    the reporter might want to put in the story mate-
    rial from the record that would question the
    allegation. But it is not necessary to do so as
    the woman's testimony is privileged. We would
    include it for the sake of fairness.
3. A city council session, like any public, official
    legislative session, is privileged. The question
    here is one of fairness. If the reporter is con-
    vinced the councilman is right - through concrete
    evidence - the charge should be used with a reply
    from Chang. If there is no evidence at all, I
    would not use the contractor's name. I would see
    if any report was made to the police.
4. The newsletter is not privileged. (See the
    Proxmire case.) Do not use.
5. The statement is not privileged. The formal
    charge, when filed, is. Do not touch the state-
    ment unless you are willing to risk a libel suit,
    should the charge not be filed.
6. Use it. Grand jury reports are privileged.

7. Avoid the issue of his institutionalization. It is not worth the risk that he could sue, and a jury could well find that his health problems were matters of privacy. Certainly, the rock star is a newsworthy person, but his addiction is a personal matter. Finally, you have no proof that the rumors are true. If they are not and he sues for libel, this would have to be defended on the ground that he is a public figure.

8. If you cannot see the file, do not use the material. It is not privileged, though an official said it is true. If you see that the record and the statement are true, then there is no question that, although the material meets the definition of matter that is libelous, it is defensible because of its truth. The question then is one of ethics. Most reputable journalists would not use the material unless it has some relevance to his candidacy.

9. You can use it if you like. It is part of an official record. The witness has invited some notoriety by testifying voluntarily. To be fair, you would want to interview him about the case.

10. Probably not. Although the lawyer may be well-known, it is difficult to class him as a public figure (see Gertz). It would be hard to prove the truth of the description, so truth as a defense is remote.

B. Ethics

1. This is a private club, not an official body. You have no legal right and little moral justification to attend. The probability is that you can dig the information out of a source. Even if you don't think you can, it is not worth a compromise of principle.

2. Most reporters would not want to insult the source
   by refusing the drink on ethical grounds. But a
   lunch should be paid for by the reporter. Is
   there a working rule--anything over a dollar or
   two should be paid for by the reporter or the
   newspaper? You might want to explore this. Most
   reporters are insulted that anyone would presume
   they can be bought for a beer or a sandwich.
3. Tell the editor. Suggest the quote be included
   in the story. Stay away from the business office. If the editor wants to take it up with
   the publisher, that is the editor's business.
   Most good editors will tell the publisher and
   say that the quote will be used. Good publishers
   will approve.
4. A much-debated subject, listening in on official
   or quasi-official bodies. A political party is
   not the same as a city council. Yet, the public
   interest is certainly involved in a meeting such
   as this one. Some reporters make "public interest" the point. They would not eavesdrop unless
   the public interest was compelling. In short,
   no absolute rule exists against eavesdropping.
   As for the use of an electronic device, that is
   considered unethical and in some cases an invasion of privacy. It opens doors to practices
   no journalist would care to contemplate: place-
   ment of bugs in committee rooms, under beds,
   in automobiles, on telephones. This is the kind
   of deception journalists are committed to expose
   when practiced by others.
5. Such records are considered private material.
   Many reporters would look at the material, but
   not use it unless a serious mistake was about
   to be made in the selection of one of the candidates. The candidates' school grades, marital
   histories, physical conditions, and like matter
   are confidential. I would say no to asking for
   the records.

6. The sports editor obviously did not want to have
    anyone on his staff compromised. Moonlighting
    by reporters used to be far more prevalent when
    wages were low and a sense of morality not yet
    developed. Generally, a reporter should not take
    money for writing or advising people or organiza-
    tions that seek coverage.

    What, then, of serving as publicity director
    for the Red Cross or the United Way? Here, the
    ethical pull of serving as a good citizen runs
    counter to the demands of the profession. There
    are powerful advocates of both positions, and
    neither is vulnerable to attack on moral grounds.
    I would not serve, but many fine journalists I
    know have done so and even run for office, with
    no compromise of their conscience or their work.

    The ASNE in 1975 replaced its Code of Ethics
    (1922) with a Statement of Principles that you
    might want to discuss with your students. In
    this situation, one of the statements may apply:

    Journalists must avoid improPriety and the appearance of impropriety as well as any conflict of interest or the appearance of conflict. They should neither accept anything nor pursue any activity that might compromise or seem to compromise their integrity.

    This statement applies to all journalists,
    but publishers seem exempt. In a study in which
    I participated of 105 New England daily news-
    papers, we found publishers who served on the
    boards of banks and were involved in business,
    politics and other activities that most reporters
    would eschew. Should publishers toe the line,
    too? You might discuss this.

7. The quick and obvious answer is that the journal-
    ist writes the truth and plays no favorites. But
    to maintain this as the virtuous course of action
    would be to ignore reality. Reporters do protect

their sources. If the misdeed is minor, a reporter will try to convince a source that the story will do no harm. If the infraction is serious, the reporter will give the piece to another reporter to write.

No reporter should protect anyone, whatever the reporter's personal interest. Some newspapers have staffers with no regular beat who are used, among other purposes, for the job of digging up material that would damage the beat reporter's relationship with sources. In other words, the reporter has a moral obligation to see to it that the story does appear, whether under the reporter's byline or another's, in one paper or another. Who does the piece and where it appears or is broadcast is not the point.

8. One way that lobbyists in an eastern state were paying off legislators was by regularly losing to them at poker games. Let's say this is not probable in the situation here. Does a reporter surrender personal friendships as the price of integrity? Many reporters would say yes, and they would certainly say that any situation in which money changes hands (except among reporters) is dangerous. Turn down the poker. Accept the invitation to play softball with the legislators.

9. The general rule about race was for many years: Don't be negative if you cannot be positive. It still is useful if by being negative is meant going out of the way to be critical or by having dual standards, one for whites, the other for minority group members. But minority groups do have problems, and the days have passed when blacks, Spanish-speaking people and the many other minorities asked that their problems be ignored. In fact, ignoring these problems--for many reasons, sometimes even in the interest of ethical journalism--has served to continue the situations that are causing distress.

For years, most big-city newspapers would not carry the fact that a large percentage of crime was being committed by minority groups. Lost in this gentleman's agreement was the fact that overwhelming numbers of the victims were minority group members. Thus, the public was uninformed about some of the tragedies of ghetto life: that it can be unsafe, unhealthy, debilitating.

The rape data should be used. I would try, in any story involving crime data, to gain perspective by interviewing people about the causes of crime, and the relationship of crime to education and to socio-economic factors. This is, of course, uncharted territory. No one can say that a, b and c cause crime. But speculations are worthy of the reporter's concern in this context.

10. Thanks, but no thanks. The reporter would expose the highway engineer who buys property in an area he knows will soon be the location of a large interchange. There is no difference here. This is a conflict of interest.

11. Print the story. The Louisville Courier-Journal ran a detailed piece by Jim Herzog, its Washington correspondent, about the paper's CIA connection. Suppose the publisher does not want to go along. What, then, is the reporter's obligation? Should the reporter leak the story to another newspaper or station? Reporters whose editors refuse to run their stories will do this. Or they will submit the piece, under a pseudonym, to another publication--sometimes at the risk of losing their jobs.

The question here is loyalty. To whom is it due? Certainly, to the employer. But there is an overriding obligation, a moral commitment to the public, to tell important truths to the people. Reporters do quit their jobs over such

matters if they feel that their truth-telling
is being blunted by policy, an editor or the
publisher. The Courier-Journal story was run
at the urging of the publisher.

12. Stay home. Or hock the family silver and go.
Avoid accepting free rides, of any kind.

13. It is difficult to regulate the heart, but young
reporters--and some not so young--have been
put into difficult situations by becoming social-
ly involved with their sources. The wise reporter casts the net elsewhere. If the attrac-
tion is considerable, then the reporter should
ask for another beat and continue the relationship. There is nothing wrong with being friendly
on office time.

14. The fate of whistle blowers is well-known: a
moment in the sun, the community's appreciation
and then no job. Often, the informant is black-
listed by industry. The reporter should be fair
to the source and describe the consequences he
or she could encounter. On the other hand, some
reporters presume that the source's informing
the reporter indicates a decision has been made
to risk the possible trouble. This viewpoint,
heard frequently in the newsroom in many situations, absolves these reporters from confronta-
tion with the moral problem. Here, you might
want to speculate with the class about the morality of stories that expose people to the public
eye, as pitying and compassionate as that gaze
may be. The reporter has a good story; the wel-
fare mother, the whistle blower or the abandoned
child usually is no better off after exposure to
public view.

15. Exhaust all appeals, up through the publisher or
owner of the station. Point out that it would be
better to run the story than allow the opposition
to publish it, for the situation cannot be kept
secret once the assessment report is made public.

If the answer is still no, the reporter has a difficult decision to make - whether to stay or look for another job. When he was dean of the School of Journalism at Columbia, Edward Barrett advised graduating students to keep in reserve for just such circumstances a "go-to-hell fund" to finance a move.

A reporter for a New Jersey newspaper was faced with a similar situation when he did a story on exclusive and exclusionary clubs in southern New Jersey. He learned that his publisher was a member and an official of a club that excluded blacks and Jews. The reporter included that fact, and the piece kicked around, upstairs and downstairs. The reporter was ready to quit over the matter, and so informed his editor. Whether his stand was responsible (the editor may have had visions of the episode appearing in a journalism review) or good sense prevailed, the story did run with the information about the publisher in it.

ASSIGNMENT

Bruce Plopper, who teaches a course in ethics at Humboldt State University, says that students are particularly bothered by the coverage of pseudo-events and by incomplete reporting. They are disturbed, he says, that the media spend so much time and space on events of minor, if any, significance, while they ignore matters that affect large numbers of people.

You might ask your students what disturbs them about the newspapers and magazines they read and the television news programs they watch. Have them bring specific examples to class.

125

C. Taste

1. I don't know any newspaper that would run a
   photograph of this sort. It is offensive, but
   so are many pictures that are published. But
   it has no point to make other than to shock the
   reader. The picture of the dead child in Columbus is shocking, perhaps sensational. But
   it can be defended as warning youngsters and
   their parents, even motorists. The yearbook
   picture has no message.
2. Students may not find much in local newspapers,
   should your area be seen as conservative in
   these matters by editors. The news magazines
   are more liberal, as are metropolitan dailies.
   Discuss this aspect of decisions about taste--
   the audience.
3. Following the interviews with your guests, try
   to have the class generalize about why they
   took the positions they did. Youth may be a
   factor, the high school editor speaking more
   liberally than the managing editor. Business
   people are generally considered more conservative than teachers or journalists. And so on.

Here are four wire service stories you may want to
discuss in class:

1. <u>Surgery</u>

   Yonkers, N.Y. - A pretty, 23-year-old woman steno-
grapher has been turned in-to a man by several operations performed at her own request, doctors at
Yonkers Professional Hos-pital reported today.

   The woman, identified as Jean Leonard, was brought
to the hospital two weeks ago for a stomach operation.

   On the operating table, doctors discovered she had
the traits of a man and a woman.

   Informed of the discov-ery, the woman said she
would rather be a man. So in the next 10 days the

126

doctors performed one major and several minor operations. The surgeons were Drs. Louis W. Martin and Charles Almond.

Upon release from the hospital, the patient changed her name to "John" and began wearing men's clothing, the doctors said.

Dr. John J. Farley, deputy city health commissioner, who confirmed the success of the operation, said he had talked to the patient Thursday and that he was "feeling swell."

He said the woman, who grew up in the community and was graduated from high school as a girl, had become a handsome man, lithe and dark haired.

The commissioner quoted John as saying that it was "somewhat embarrassing" to meet former friends who knew him as a girl.

"I guess I'll have to go South and start a new life," John was quoted.

Sex change operations are no longer considered distasteful. In fact, they are hardly as newsworthy as they used to be. Here, the question is use of the patient's name. It probably should not be used.

2. Stab

Urgent
    1st Lead Slaying.
New York, Nov. 4 - Wei Huan Key, 27, Chinese United Nations clerk, took Mrs. Blanche Kolyak, 33, Bulgarian-born Voice of America translator, to see the ballet "Sleeping Beauty," gave her a flowered oriental gown and finally stabbed her to death early today.

Then he plunged the $4\frac{1}{2}$-inch blade of a hunting knife six times into his own chest and lay down beside her nude body with his hands folded calmly across his chest to await death.

Their bodies were found on one of twin beds in a room of an upper Broadway hotel by a bell captain who went to investigate why the telephone had been off the hook for several hours.

Police were investigating many angles. A search of Wei's room in the Queens YMCA turned up a penciled note which said: "We are that way because American men give us everything but love."

127

Lurid and perhaps too detailed, but not beyond the bonds of good taste. The cryptic note seems to make the story. The question seems to be. Would you use it in Dubuque? Mine is probably a minority opinion, but after cutting some of the details, I would use the note because it is striking.

3. Massage

Tuckahoe, N.Y. May 5 - A 17-year-old six-foot blond accused Michael Donne, 34, substitute mail carrier, of giving her reducing treatments in the nude after promising to promote her in a beauty contest.

Donne, father of three children, was released on $1,000 bail on a charge of second-degree rape. He denied the charge.

Josephine Schugar, statuesque Bronx school girl, said Donne took pictures of her in the nude, then gave her massage treatments.

Miss Schugar said Donne became friendly with her friend, Sandra Ross, an amateur photography fan, while delivering mail. Miss Ross introduced him to Miss Schugar and Donne allegedly offered to promote her in a beauty contest.

He first took pictures of her in modest poses in his home, then persuaded her to disrobe, she charged. He then took several more pictures and gave her a massage treatment. When she returned to look at the developed pictures, he gave her another treatment, she charged. Miss Schugar told her parents, who reported the incident to police.

Police sent Miss Schugar to pose for Donne again, then raided his studio while she was there. The raiders seized a number of pictures including those of other girls, a reducing roller and a quantity of Epsom salts, which they said Donne used in reducing baths for his protegees.

John Heard, investigator for the Westchester county sheriff's office, said he was investigating reports that Donne interviewed 20 other girls in a similar manner.

This one seems to go on and on and obviously needs cutting, but should you use the 17-year-old's name, Josephine Schugar? This brings up the issue of using the names of victims of sex crimes. Some women demand that they be treated equally, and that women's names be used. Most editors decline. I do not think it is chauvinism. Certainly, there is a difference between the victim of a robbery and of a rape. But see what your students think.

4. Incest

Wichita, Kan., Dec. 13 - A 50-year-old father of six children was held in jail today on an open charge after his arrest on complaint of a daughter, 12.

Police Sgt. Rex Betz said that the daughter, Ann Jones, alleged her father, Clarence E. Jones, had forced her to have sexual relations with him.

Jones denied the charge. Betz said a physician examined the girl and found she had had sexual relations.

Jones's wife, Mildred, and the five other children, are living in Little Rock, Ark., police said.

Jones and Ann were living together here and the girl was in intermediate school.

Do you use this anywhere but in Wichita? Probably not. And in Wichita do you use the child's name? No. But if you use the father's name, the child's identity will probably be known. I would junk the item completely.

You may want to have your students comment on some of my conclusions about (1) the use of the phrase <u>fucking narc</u> in the textbook, (2) the Larry Price photos of the executions in Liberia and (3) the picture of the dead child the Columbus paper ran. As I remarked at the outset, there are not too many absolutes in these areas. However, do not allow students to say they simply did not like the language or the pictures.

If their reasons are interesting, send them on. I'd like to use them in subsequent editions.

INDEX

Acne 32
Analysis 51
Answer 19
Appointees 113
Appreciation 109
Arrested 92
Artful 67
Astrology 81

Belmont 12
Bicycle Trip 14
Bids 52
Bite 96
Brush-off 14
Bus 52

Cab 42
Calendar 54
Cecil 82
Center 19
Changes 12
Coach 68
Cold 114
Cookies 95
Council 80
Craftsman 17
Crime Reports 95
Criticism 75

Daredevil 54
Dispute 3
District Attorney 113
Drive 13
Driving 82
Drowning 93
Drugs 91

Ethics 119

Fire 2
Flies 73

Galloway 75
Gas 13
Goals 36
Golfers 11
Growth 27
Guns 14

Hoofer 70
Hot Line 45

Ibbotson 97
Ignorance 31

Lakes 71
Laundromat 2
Libel and Privacy 118
Lifesaver 55
Lobby 111
Longo 99
Loser 105

Mail 4
Memorial 2
Merit 112
Missing 53

SKILL DRILLS